I0834301

the WISE FATHER INSTRUCTS HIS SON *on* SEXUAL SIN *and* GOSPEL HOPE

An Exposition *of* Proverbs 7

CURTIS BRAUN

LUCIDBOOKS

The Wise Father Instructs His Son on Sexual Sin and Gospel Hope
An Exposition of Proverbs 7

Copyright © 2026 by Curtis Braun

Published by Lucid Books in Houston, TX
www.LucidBooks.com

All rights reserved. No part of this publication may be reproduced, stored in a retrieval system, or transmitted in any form by any means, electronic, mechanical, photocopy, recording, or otherwise, without the prior permission of the publisher, except as provided for by USA copyright law.

Unless otherwise indicated, scripture quotations are taken from the ESV® Bible (The Holy Bible, English Standard Version®), copyright © 2001 by Crossway, a publishing ministry of Good News Publishers. Used by permission. All rights reserved.

Scripture quotations marked (NASB) are taken from the (NASB®) New American Standard Bible®, Copyright © 1960, 1971, 1977, 1995, 2020 by The Lockman Foundation. Used by permission. All rights reserved. www.lockman.org

Paperback ISBN: 979-8-90344-010-8
eISBN: 979-8-90344-011-5

Special Sales: Most Lucid Books titles are available in special quantity discounts. Custom imprinting or excerpting can also be done to fit special needs. Contact Lucid Books at Info@LucidBooks.com

Dedication

To Laura, Pax Emmanuel, and Keryx Kyrie: I love you all very much. Remember, all who desire to live a godly life in Christ Jesus will be persecuted. Do not be ashamed of the Lord and His gospel. Stand firm in the faith and let nothing move you. Be strong in the Lord and His Word. Love the Lord your God with all your heart, and with all your soul, and with all your mind, and with all your strength. Seek the Lord with all your heart and serve Him only. Be steadfast, immovable, always abounding in the work of the Lord. Always give yourself fully to the work of the Lord because you know that your labor in the Lord is not in vain. Whatever you do, whether you eat or drink, do it all for the glory of the Lord. Lastly, repent and put your faith in the Lord Jesus Christ.

To Keryx and Pax: One day I will give you these instructions when you're old enough and able to be instructed in these truths. You must understand that your father is not the hero of this book. In fact, there is only one Hero in the book, the Lord Jesus Christ. He is the one who saved my soul from a wretched life of sexual immorality and adultery. I was not a Christian who just fell into deep transgression. I was a lost and hell-bound church goer who was in bondage to sin. Therefore, I exhort you to trust in the Lord with all your heart and lean not on your own understanding. In all your ways acknowledge Him and He will make straight your paths. Be not wise in your own eyes; fear the LORD, and turn away from evil.

My beloved sons, keep my words, treasure up my commandments within you. Keep my commandments and live. Keep my teaching as the apple of your eye. Bind them on your fingers and write them on the tablet of your heart. Say to wisdom, "You are my sister," and call insight your intimate friend to keep you from the forbidden woman, from the adulteress with her smooth words and from sexual sin. Deny yourself, take up your cross, and follow Christ.

Contents

Preface

Writing a book about fathers and parents teaching their sons the dangers of sexual sin and the need for the gospel may appear strange and even unwise. Discussing sexual sin is often viewed as uncomfortable and embarrassing. However, the Bible is not ashamed or bashful about warning how mankind is tempted and overcome by sexual sin and the adulterer or adulteress. The Bible also speaks in detail on the consequences of this sin and gives clear commands on how we are to abstain or flee from sexual sin and how we are to repent when necessary. The Bible is also very clear that it is both the father and mother's biblical duty to instruct their children on the dangers of sexual sin.

I have spoken with many pastors who are afraid to address, preach on, or teach on this subject, which is considered off-limits in sermons and Bible studies in the church. Common excuses include, "That's not something you share with the congregation," or "It may be a problem, but I just deal with it privately in counseling." Such thinking is unbiblical and alien to Scripture as we see that King Solomon's father, King David, and his mother, Bathsheba instructed him about the adulteress and sexual temptation when he was young (Proverbs 4:3–4, 6:20). Additionally, Proverbs chapters 2, 5, 6, and 7 include warnings regarding sexual sin; clearly, the triune God inspired King Solomon to give strong and descriptive warnings regarding this sin. Therefore, the argument or excuse that this sin should not be preached about or made known in the church is unbiblical, cowardly, and ignorant.

I am writing on this topic because not only is it neglected in the churches but it is also neglected in schools that claim to be Christian. I attended a Lutheran high school in Minnesota where various forms of sexual immorality were practiced by many students. This included the young men discussing and watching pornography, sexual immorality and fornication between boyfriends and girlfriends in the student population as well as perverse, crude, and sexually charged discussions and joking among the students.

There were opportunities for the responsible adults to confront these issues. For instance, a fifteen- to twenty-minute chapel was held every day, led by a teacher or a pastor from one of ten churches nearby. However, was the topic of sexual immorality ever taught? Was the salvation of those who were actively and unrepentantly viewing pornography ever questioned? Was the salvation of the young men and women who were unrepentantly sexually active ever questioned? Was there ever a call for students to examine themselves to see if they were in the faith (1 Corinthians 13:5)? Was sexual sin ever dealt with in light of the gospel? The answer to each of these questions is a resounding no. I surmise that this high school experience would be on par with that of many other schools that bear the name "Christian," and I would expect that this type of activity may be equal or worse in non-Christian schools.

I have also heard about men of all ages engaging in different types of sexual sin within the church; these are men who unrepentantly engage in sexual immorality and believe themselves to be Christians. Such men claim they've never committed adultery, but their children find dirty magazines in their tool sheds; some are unfaithful to their wives and minimize their sin and by saying, "I lacked integrity." There are unmarried men and women who live together unrepentantly and attend church who say, "I'm justified by faith and not works." Some pastors claim that unrepentant sexually immoral churchgoers are saved because they have been baptized and have the Holy Spirit; men and teenagers secretly indulge in pornography. The church is to be the pillar and ground of the truth, and it is manifestly clear that the Lord wants this instruction and warning regarding sexual sin to be taught in His church (1 Timothy 3:15, 1 Thessalonians 4:3, Revelation 2:14, 2:20).

Not only is this to be a book on the dangers of sexual sin and the mandate to teach one's children about these matters, but this book was also written to proclaim the gospel. It is no good if someone is an upstanding husband or wife, but doesn't savingly believe in the Lord Jesus Christ. It does a person no good if they learn about sexual sin, avoid sexual sin, yet never come to true repentance and a saving knowledge of Christ. Many people have strong marriages, yet do not savingly know Christ and are self-deceived (Matthew 7:21–23). Therefore, the last chapter in this book is devoted to presenting the gospel. Not only are parents to warn their children of sexual sin, but they are also to teach their children the gospel in hopes that their children may be saved. The father and mother can show their children that the Lord is willing and able to save the sexually immoral, adulterers, homosexuals, and fornicators (1 Corinthians 6:9–11). The father can show the son that the Lord is willing to wash, sanctify, and justify the worst of sinners. The gospel is the only hope for the adulterer, the adulteress, the homosexual, the porn-enslaved sinner, the fornicator, and all mankind enslaved to sin. I am also compelled to present the gospel because there are many false gospels in modern Christianity: baptismal regeneration, sacramental conversion and salvation, prosperity gospel, easy-believism, presumptive regeneration, works-based salvation, and more. It is my heart's desire that the Lord be glorified by proclaiming the true gospel and that sinners be saved and the saints be built up.

Finally, I heartily acknowledge that the Lord Jesus Christ saved me from a life of adultery, pornography, lying, and manipulation. Though I was in the church, I was not a part of Christ's kingdom; I attended church on Sunday, but I was a hypocrite of the worst kind. Though I knew the Lord's prayer, the Apostle's Creed, the Ten Commandments, and more, I did not know the Lord. The Lord is willing and able to save the most perverted, hypocritical, corrupt, vile, wretched, polluted, and idolatrous sinner of whom I could be considered foremost. The Lord was gracious to cause me to be born again, grant me repentance, and grant me saving faith. Though I desired to take my life and end it, the Lord gave me new life, regeneration. Along with the Corinthian believers, this is my testimony:

> *Or do you not know that the unrighteous will not inherit the kingdom of God? Do not be deceived: neither the* ***sexually immoral, nor idolaters, nor adulterers,*** *nor men who practice homosexuality, nor thieves,* ***nor the greedy,*** *nor drunkards, nor revilers, nor swindlers will inherit the kingdom of God. And such were some of you. But you were washed, you were sanctified, you were justified in the name of the Lord Jesus Christ and by the Spirit of our God.*
>
> —1 Corinthians 6:9–11(emphasis added)

Chapter 1

The Father Instructs and Commands the Son; the Son's Responsibility to Hear and Obey His Father

My son, keep my words and treasure up my commandments with you.

—Proverbs 7:1

In this chapter, we will examine the first five verses of Proverbs chapter 7. As we begin our exposition of Proverbs 7, it is helpful to see that in the first four verses, the father gives the son nine commands that come in staccato fashion. It is the duty of the father to give these commands to his son, and it is the son's responsibility to listen and obey his father. Below are the nine commands that appear in the first four verses of Proverbs 7:

- **Keep** my words. (v. 1)
- **Treasure up** my commandments within you. (v. 1)

- **Keep** my commandments. (v. 2)
- **Live**. (v. 2)
- **Keep** my teaching as the apple of your eye. (2)
- **Bind** them on your fingers. (v. 3)
- **Write** them on the tablet of your heart. (v. 3)
- **Say** to wisdom, "You are my sister." (v. 4)
- **Call** insight your intimate friend. (v. 4)

Before we get started, there are a couple of points that need to be made. First, though the father is talking about the dangers of the adulteress, I refer to the adulteress as "sexual sin" and an "adulterer" throughout the book. I believe that the reader will see how sexual sin and the adulterer can be used interchangeably with the adulteress without altering the meaning and intent of Scripture. Additionally, throughout the text I will use the father as the instructor and the son as the recipient of the instruction. However, we'll see that the instructor is not limited to only fathers, and instruction is not limited to sons. This instruction can and should be given by mothers, and this instruction can and should be received by daughters. With this in mind, let's begin our exposition of Proverbs 7:1–5.

The Father's Duty to Instruct His Son on Sexual Sin

Before we look at the commands, the first thing we should notice is Scripture's mandate is that fathers are to teach their children of the dangers of sexual sin. We see this as the father begins Proverbs chapter 7 by addressing his son. Fathers are not to be apathetic, indifferent, or negligent in instructing their sons regarding the dangers of sexual sin. Scripture gives no exception clause to fathers because they may feel uncomfortable, embarrassed, see other fathers refuse to instruct their sons, or any of the myriads of reasons that a father may give for not instructing and warning their sons. Scripture is very clear that instructing the son is the job, duty, and mandate of the father. Yes, there are fathers who want to teach their son how to "turn a wrench," "swing a club," "play an instrument," "learn a hobby," and many other things. However, where is the biblical father that will teach and warn his son of sexual sin? Sadly, it is almost non-existent in modern Christianity. For a father to neglect to warn his son of the dangers of sexual sin is for a father to neglect his duty as a father. Scripture is very concerned about the dangers of sexual sin. The opening seven chapters of Proverbs warn of the adulterous woman and sexual sin four times (Proverbs 2:16, 5:1–23, 6:20–35, 7:1–27). Therefore, we should understand that the repeated warnings given by Scripture, Solomon, and the Holy Spirit are intended to catch our attention in order that we may heed this wisdom. In these first seven chapters, we are warned that the adulteress must be avoided (Proverbs 5:8), that her outward beauty must not be desired (Proverbs 6:24), and that her footsteps lead to death (Proverbs 5:5). It would serve all fathers well to understand that instructing their sons regarding this sin is necessary and good. Not only this, but if a father refuses to instruct his son or finds his son falling into sexual sin and does not warn or discipline him, Scripture says that, in effect, the father or parent hates their son or child (Proverbs 13:24).

Second, we should see that it's not only the job of the father to instruct his son regarding the dangers of sexual sin, but we also see that the father must teach his son with all diligence. In Deuteronomy 6:5–7, we get this command on how parents are to instruct their children (emphasis added):

> *You shall love the Lord your God with all your heart and with all your soul and with all your might. And these words that I command you today shall be on your heart. You* ***shall teach them diligently to your children****, and shall talk of them when you sit in your house, and when you walk by the way, and when you lie down, and when you rise.*

In Deuteronomy 6:7, we see that parents are to diligently teach their children the Lord's commands and to love Him with all their heart, soul, and might. The phrase "*teach them diligently*" comes from the word *shanan*, which can mean to "sharpen," "inculcate," or "teach diligently." This word portrays a blade or arrow being deliberately honed and sharpened so that the point will strike true; *shanan* also communicates that this is more than casual instruction. In fact, this type of diligent teaching is consistent, intentional, and thorough. This instruction is a far cry from modern parenting advice or from fathers who say, "It's time to have a discussion on the birds and the bees," or "It's time to sit down and have 'the talk,'" or "I'm not comfortable discussing these things.'" Such thinking is alien and foreign to Scripture, which exhorts parents to diligently, consistently, intentionally, and thoroughly instruct their children about the Lord and His commands and, as we see in Proverbs 7, the dangers of sexual sin.

As we just mentioned, the father is to be consistent, intentional, and deliberate in that he continually gives the same message and warning regarding sexual sin. This means the message regarding the consequences, deceptiveness, dangers, and shunning of sin is to be taught. The father is to be intentional in that he is purposeful to warn and instruct his son at the appropriate times and in the course and flow of life. Likewise, the father is to thoroughly instruct his son that sexual intimacy is to be honored and enjoyed in the context of a marriage between a husband and a wife and that any sexual activity outside of marriage is sinful and disobedient (Proverbs 5:18–19, Matthew 19:4–9, Hebrews 13:4). A father must be thorough in his instruction to his son. However, being thorough does not mean being graphic, explicit, or perverted in a way that damages the tender conscience of the son or causes him to stumble into sin (Proverbs 4:3, Matthew 18:5–9). The father is to instruct his son in a way that protects the innocence and tenderness of his son.

From Scripture, we see that it is also the mother's responsibility to teach her son or children regarding the dangers of sexual sin. We see this in Proverbs 6:20 and 24 which say, "*My son, keep your father's commandment, and* ***forsake***

***not your mother's teaching**. . . to preserve you from the evil woman, from the smooth tongue of the adulteress*" (emphasis added). From this, we see that Scripture commands that mothers instruct their sons regarding sexual sin. Mothers are not to avoid instructing their sons regarding sexual sin; rather, they are to instruct their sons, and the sons are to not forsake their mother's teaching. Let's remember that Solomon wrote the book of Proverbs and that his mother was Bathsheba, and his father was King David who were both guilty of committing adultery (2 Samuel 11). If two parents who committed adultery instructed their son on the dangers of sexual sin, how much more should Christian parents instruct their sons and daughters of these dangers? No parent is above this command, and no child is so free from sin that they should not be warned and instructed.

We should also seek to understand when this instruction should take place in the life of a child. In Proverbs 4:3–4, we see that Solomon was being instructed at an age when he was tender as it says, "*When I was a son with my father, **tender**, the only one in the sight of my mother, he taught me and said to me, "Let your heart hold fast my words; keep my commandments, and live*" (emphasis added). The word *tender* comes from the original word *rak*, which can mean inexperienced, weak, frail, or gentle. In 1 Chronicles 22:5, David says that Solomon is young (*na`ar*) and inexperienced or tender (*rak)* when he was instructed. The word *na`ar* can be used to describe someone from the age of infancy to adolescence. From the context of 1 Chronicles 22, it is clear that Solomon is certainly not a baby because even though he is young (*na`ar)* and tender (*rak)*, David charges him with building the temple of God (1 Chronicles 22:6–19). Therefore, in Proverbs 4:3–4, we can surmise that Solomon was instructed of the dangers of sexual sin by his father at an age when he had intellectual capacity to reason, when he was teachable, and when he was able to comprehend his father's instruction.

So how would a father discern at what age to instruct his son on sexual sin? If a father home schools his son and can control the amount of sexual immorality his son is exposed to, should the father begin his instruction at a later age? Perhaps. If a father has a son who has been abused or exposed to deviant, wicked, and perverse acts as young as age six, should the father begin his instruction earlier? Perhaps. If a father has a son who has been exposed to wicked and perverse material on the internet as young as age seven, should the father begin his instruction earlier? Perhaps. It would seem appropriate to begin instructing one's son at an age when the son has intellectual capacity and teachability to comprehend the father's instruction. Instruction could also begin sooner depending on the son's exposure to wicked and immoral acts or deviant material. This answer as to when to begin instructing a child of these dangers may seem vague, but let's remember that the father is to be wise and discerning in how he teaches his son on the dangers of sexual sin while protecting his son's innocence and not causing him to stumble into sin.

Keep the Father's Instruction

The son's first duty in response to the father's instruction is to "*keep my words.*" This command is written in the imperative, which simply means that this is a command. It is not an idea, suggestion, recommendation, or opinion. This is a direct command from the father to the son, and the only appropriate response from the son is obedience. The word *keep* comes from the original word *shamar*, which conveys the idea of guarding, protecting, or observing. This word doesn't convey the idea of a begrudging or a half-hearted obedience. Rather, this word carries the idea of obedience fueled by love. We see this in Exodus 20:6 when the Lord is giving the Ten Commandments and says, "*but showing steadfast love to thousands of* ***those who love me and keep my commandments***" (emphasis added). Love and obedience are inextricably tied together, but it is love that precedes obedience, and it is love that leads to obedience. Therefore, love is the root, and obedience is the fruit that proceeds from love. Jesus says this very same truth in John 14:15: "*If you love me, you will keep my commandments.*" In Jesus's statement in John 14:15, we see that love precedes obedience and that obedience proceeds from love. The Apostle John reiterates this truth in his first letter when he says this in 1 John 5:3: "*For* ***this is the love of God****, that* ***we keep his commandments****. And his commandments are not burdensome*" (emphasis added). Thus, when the father commands his son to keep his words as it relates to sexual sin, the father is demonstrating love for his son because he knows that sexual sin is dangerous and leads to death. Likewise, when the son keeps his father's words regarding the adulterous woman, the son shows love for his father by keeping his father's commands. This is God's pattern for the family. It is the father who loves the Lord and who instructs his son because he loves the son. When the son becomes a father, he will instruct his son out of love and obedience for the Lord and the love he has for his son. This is part of the Lord's plan for marriage and raising godly offspring (Malachi 2:15). Thus, the command to keep the father's words imply that the son keeps the father's instruction out of love for his father.

Additionally, when the son obeys his father, he is to honor his father. This command to honor one's father is captured in the Ten Commandments and in the New Testament. Ephesians 6:1–2 says, "*Children,* ***obey*** *your parents in the Lord, for this is right. '****Honor*** *your father and mother' (this is the first commandment with a promise*)'" (emphasis added). The word *obey* comes from *hupakouó*, which means "to hear under" or figuratively "to listen in order to conform." The word *honor* comes from the word *timaó*, which means to revere, prize, or value; *timaó* conveys the idea of giving someone personal esteem, value, and preciousness. Thus, we see that the New Testament carries the same connotation as we see in Proverbs; that is, obedience is not to be done sluggishly or unwillingly. Rather, obedience comes from the heart, and it is to be the fruit that comes from the root of loving and honoring one's father. Honor is to precede obedience, and obedience is the fruit that is to proceed from a heart that reveres and honors one's father. This is how the son is to keep his father's words. Thus, the son is to keep the father's words because he loves, trusts, and honors his father and seeks to love and obey the Lord.

Treasure the Father's Commands

The second command to the son is to treasure up the father's commands. The phrase *treasure up* comes from the original word *tsaphan*, which conveys the idea of purposeful concealment to protect, preserve, or treasure. It conveys an internalization and meditation on God's Word to spiritually form one's conscience, affections, and obedience. Additionally, this command is given in the imperfect tense, which simply means that this is an incomplete action and implies that the son is going to continue to treasure up the father's command in the present and the future. It's important to note that because the phrase *treasure up* is written in the imperfect tense, it assumes that the father continually teaches and instructs his son. The father's instruction is not just a one-time lecture. Rather, Scripture teaches us that ongoing diligent and purposeful instruction is meant to shape the thoughts, affections, and character of the son. Just as the son continues to treasure up the father's instruction, so the father is persistent and intentional in instructing his son. It is a picture of the father giving his son precious jewels of godly wisdom, and the son hoarding, protecting, and preserving this wisdom as precious and valuable.

When the father commands the son to "*treasure up*" his commandments, the purpose of treasuring up his commandments and instructions is to form the son's conscience. It is important to note that the conscience is the faculty by which individuals discern ethical and moral choices, which reflect what is in the heart. The conscience discerns what is morally good and bad; the conscience either accuses or excuses one's actions. The conscience can either be made sensitive or dulled by the morality or ethical standard around it.

For example, if someone is told that committing adultery is only the physical act of adultery between a married spouse and someone the individual is not married to, then the conscience is informed that adultery is merely physical. Pornography, fornication, lustful thoughts, and visiting houses of ill-repute could be perceived as acceptable if the conscience hasn't been informed that these other acts are sinful acts of sexual immorality. If the conscience is informed that adultery is looking at a woman with lustful intent, then the conscience has been made more sensitive to a higher level of godly morality (Matthew 5:28). Sharpening and making the conscience more sensitive and making it aware of sin is one of the reasons the son is to treasure up the father's commandments. The father's aim is not to water down and trivialize sin for this would dull his son's conscience to sin. Rather, the father is sharpening and making the son's conscience sensitive and tender to sin. The father is helping the son see sin for what it really is, rebellion and wickedness against God.

Additionally, treasuring up the father's commandments is to form the son's affections. The instruction is to help the son love the things that God loves and hate the things that God hates. By treasuring up the father's commands, the son is to love and seek wisdom (Proverbs 2:4); this wisdom will be stored up and protected in the son's heart, and this knowledge will be pleasant to his soul and guard and protect him from the way of evil, perverted speech, the ways of darkness, and from the adulterous woman and sexual sin (Proverbs 2:10–16). The father's highest purpose isn't to merely make his son a moral person and impart good manners; it is to impart the knowledge of God to his son in order that his son will possess the fear of the Lord (Proverbs 1:7). What is the fear of the Lord? The fear of the Lord is best understood as a heart or state of mind that knows and understands the Lord as He is; responds in reverence toward God; and exchanges one's own attitudes, will, feelings, and deeds for God's will.

Keep the Father's Commands and Live

> *Keep my commandments and live; keep my teaching as the apple of your eye.*
>
> —Proverbs 7:2

The father's immense love for the son is revealed in the third and fourth commands: Keep the father's command and live. Both verbs are written in the imperative, which simply means that they are commands. The father's commandments and instructions are given for the purposes of teaching the son to live a life in the fear of the Lord and keeping him from death. This instruction is given to guard the path of the son and keep him in safety (Proverbs 2:8), to impart the wisdom of the Lord and give the son knowledge and understanding (Proverbs 2:6), and to teach him to follow every good path (Proverbs 2:9). This instruction is a matter of life and death. It is true that all sin is devastating. However, as mentioned earlier, the father is deliberate and intentional in warning his son of the adulterous woman in Proverbs chapter 2, 5, 6, and 7. Therefore, we can be sure that the father wants the son to beware and avoid the disastrous entrapments that come from adultery and sexual sin.

But what is the penalty for adultery and sexual sin? Why would the father say that by keeping his commandments, his son will live? The father lays out the consequences of committing sexual sin and adultery in Proverbs 5 and 6. Consequences include the loss of a good name and honor (Proverbs 5:9, 22:1), loss of possessions or indebtedness (Proverbs 5:10, 6:31), lifelong regret and potential irreversible disease (Proverbs 5:11), destruction of one's soul (Proverbs 6:32), dishonor (Proverbs 6:33), wounds (Proverbs 6:33), reproach (Proverbs 6:33), and the wrath of the adulteress's husband (Proverbs 6:34–35).

In the Old Testament there was also the potential consequence of death. If a man committed adultery with another man's wife, both the man and the adulteress could be put to death (Deuteronomy 22:22). If a betrothed virgin had sexual intimacy with another man, both the young woman and the man would be stoned (Deuteronomy 22:23–24). Not only were there the temporal consequences and the threat of death, but there was also the devastating consequence of dying in one's sin. In Proverbs 5:22 as the father is warning his son of the consequences of adultery, he says, "*The iniquities of the wicked ensnare him, and he is held fast in the cords of his sin.*" What does it mean to be held fast in the cords of sin? The most devastating consequence of living in unrepentant sexual sin is being ensnared, held fast, entrapped, and dying in one's sin without coming to true repentance and faith in the Lord Jesus Christ. There is a saying that captures the devastating consequences of sin: "Sin will take you further than you ever wanted to go, keep you longer than you ever wanted to stay, and cost you more than you ever thought you would pay." We'll see later that the father pictures falling into the adulteress' trap and sexual sin as going down to Sheol and the chambers of death (Proverbs 7:27). The father instructs his son because he loves his son, and so he tells his son to keep his commandments and live, not die!

Love the Father's Commands

The father's fifth command makes it clear that the son is to keep the father's commands; that is, he is to highly esteem and protect the father's instruction. So, what does it mean when the father tells the son to keep his commandments as the apple of his eye? In the original language, the word *apple* comes from the word *iyshown*, which can mean the little man of the eye or the pupil or ball. The little man of the eye comes from the idea that when you look someone in the eye, you can see your own reflection, which is the little man. Additionally, the eye is an extremely sensitive part of the body. As we know, tremendous damage can be done if the eye is exposed to bacteria, foreign material such as dirt, any form of blunt trauma, prolonged exposure to direct sunlight, and so on. Because the eye is so important, people go to great lengths to protect their eyes from being injured; the phrase used in this verse points to the idea of protecting that which is valuable. In other words, this verse is saying, "keep my teaching and intensely guard it as valuable, precious, and as knowledge that must be preserved at all costs." The father is giving his son valuable godly wisdom that is to protect his son from the adulterous woman and sexual sin. The father knows that the adulterous woman uses smooth words (Proverbs 6:24, 7:5), that her speech is deceptive (Proverbs 5:3), and that she uses her looks and mannerisms to seduce (Proverbs 6:25). The father wants these commands to be regarded, valued, and esteemed as precious because he knows of the deceitfulness of sexual sin and how the devil and the adulterous woman twist that which is good to that which is bad. They turn marriage into adultery. They sever marriages rather than work to strengthen and cleave the husband and wife together. They turn physical beauty into a means for seduction. They turn honest speech into deceitful language. They turn love into lust. They are skilled in deception. Therefore, the father commands his son to highly esteem and protect his instruction.

Apply the Father's Commands

> *Bind them on your fingers; write them on the tablet of your heart.*
>
> —Proverbs 7:3

According to the sixth and seventh commands, it is the son's duty to apply God's instructions throughout the course of everyday life and to internalize his instruction. The verb for *bind* and *write* are both written in the imperative, which means they are commands. When the father tells his son to "bind them on your fingers," he is calling the son to be intentional in fastening these spiritual realities and teachings to his life as a continual reminder that all aspects of his life—body and soul—are to be lived according to the will of God. By instructing his son to bind the instructions to his hand, the father is telling the son that he needs to anchor these truths into his life in such a way that he resists sin and temptation. These truths are to be anchored and fastened onto the son's hands in such a way that they affect the son's intellect, affections, conscience, and volition. Just as the son is to purposefully bind these instructions on his hand, he is to be purposeful in thinking and living according to the instruction he has received from his father. These instructions are to show the son where and how to walk in righteousness (Proverbs 6:22). They are to speak to the son and be a living instruction that guides and protects him (Proverbs 6:22). They are to be a lamp that guides in the way of righteousness and reveals darkness, error, and sin (Proverbs 6:23). This is what it means for the son to bind his father's instruction on his fingers.

Not only is the father to instruct his son to bind these teachings on his hands, but the father is also to be a living model of what he teaches. We see this in Deuteronomy 6:5–8:

> *You shall love the Lord your God with all your heart and with all your soul and with all your might. And* ***these words that I command you today shall be on your heart****. You shall teach them diligently to your children, and shall talk of them when you sit in your house, and when you walk by the way, and when you lie down, and when you rise.* ***You shall bind them as a sign on your hand****, and they shall be as frontlets between your eyes*"" (emphasis added).

Here, we see that the father is also to bind the Lord's commands on his hands and on his heart. The father is not to be ignorant of Scripture. The father is to fear the Lord and purposefully fasten the Lord's commands on his hands to apply them to his life. The father is not to be a teaching hypocrite who instructs his son with godly wisdom but lives contrary to the teaching. He is not to be a man who instructs his son to avoid sexual sin but then has a secret life of indulgence in pornography. No, he is to let the Lord's commands and instruction form his own conscience, affections, and will.

The father is to be a living imitator of the Lord Jesus Christ who talks about the Lord's precepts when he is at home with his son, as he is going through the course of life, early when the child rises, and when the child lies down to sleep. So, not only is the son to bind the father's commands on his hands, but the father is also to bind the Lord's commands on his hands.

Meditate and Internalize the Father's Commands

The seventh command is for the son to write the father's instruction on the tablet of his heart; this word picture carries the idea of engraving on stone. In fact, the word *tablet* comes from the original word *luwach*, which could be a tablet of stone, wood or metal. Just as the son is to fasten the instruction on his hands, he is also to engrave the instructions on his heart. This is a picture of purposeful, intentional, and careful engraving. This is not taking a sledgehammer and knocking down walls and pillars. Rather, this is a picture of the son purposefully, skillfully, and diligently etching the father's commands on his heart. This is a picture of internalizing and meditating on the father's instruction with the intention of obeying it. Additionally, in Hebrew, the heart is the center of one's being; it is not merely the home of one's affections, but also the seat of the will and moral purpose. The condition of one's heart determines one's influence. Proverbs 4:23 says, "*Watch over your heart with all diligence, for from it flow the springs of life*" (NASB). The command to write the father's teachings on the tablet of the son's heart pictures the son's purposeful internalization and meditation of his father's commands to obey his father from the heart. The father wants the son to internalize his instructions so the son will find favor and good success in the sight of God and man (Proverbs 3:3–4). The father's priority is that the son will come to a saving knowledge and true repentance in the Lord Jesus Christ as written in Proverbs 3:5–7:

> *Trust in the Lord with all your heart, and do not lean on your own understanding. In all your ways acknowledge him, and he will make straight your paths. Be not wise in your own eyes; fear the Lord, and turn away from evil.*

When the son sees sexually charged images or media, the instructions that he has written on the tablet of his heart would say, "Gouge out your eyes and abstain from this filth!" When the son sees a flirtatious and seductive woman who is pushing physical boundaries, the instructions that he has bound on his hands would say, "Run for your life!"

Not only is the son to write the father's instruction on the tablet of his heart, but as we learned earlier in Deuteronomy 6:5–7, the father is to have the Lord's commands on his own heart. The father is to also internalize the Lord's commands and walk faithfully and obediently before the Lord. The father is not to be a religious hypocrite by teaching his son the Lord's commands regarding sexual sin and then flirting with other women, being unguarded in his speech with other women, viewing pornography, searching for images of other women, creating emotional connections with other women, inappropriately texting other women, cultivating sexual sins in his own heart, and so on. No, the father is to be an example and imitator of Christ to his son by engraving the Lord's commands on his own heart and following the Lord.

Build a Personal Relationship with the Father's Godly Wisdom and Commands

> *Say to wisdom, "You are my sister," and call insight your intimate friend.*
>
> —Proverbs 7:4

The eighth and ninth commands call for the son to develop a personal relationship and loyalty with his wisdom. The command for the son to call wisdom his sister is written in the imperative, which means that this is a command. But what does it mean to call wisdom one's sister? The father is purposefully commanding the son to call wisdom his sister because this invokes familial ties. These familial ties depict a relationship characterized by friendship, covenantal bonds of loyalty, and intimate knowledge. The father is not commanding that wisdom be a stranger, a foreigner, or an acquaintance. Rather, he is commanding his son to befriend wisdom, to be loyal to wisdom, and to deeply and intimately know wisdom.

This call to know godly wisdom runs across the book of Proverbs. In fact, the book opens with Solomon saying in Proverbs 1:2, "*To* ***know*** *wisdom and instruction, to understand words of insight*" (emphasis added). Solomon tells his son to make his ear attentive to wisdom and incline his heart to understanding (Proverbs 2:2). He calls his son to seek wisdom and understanding as precious like seeking silver and hidden treasure (Proverbs 2:4). He promises that wisdom and knowledge will teach him righteousness, justice, equity, and every good path (Proverbs 2:9). Thus, the father has consistently told his son that he is to intimately know wisdom for myriads of reasons. In the verses that follow, the father tells his son these truths about wisdom:

- The one who finds wisdom will be blessed; it is more precious and desirable than silver or gold and precious jewels (Proverbs 3:13–15).
- Wisdom's ways are pleasant and peaceful (Proverbs 3:17).
- Wisdom comes from the Lord and by it, the earth was created (Proverbs 3:19–20).
- Wisdom will keep the son from stumbling, and the Lord will be his confidence (Proverbs 3:23, 26).
- If he loves wisdom, wisdom will guard him (Proverbs 4:6).

- The son is to highly prize wisdom, and wisdom will exalt him (Proverbs 4:8).
- Wisdom and instruction will be the son's life if he guards and holds on to her (Proverbs 4:13).
- Wisdom is to fear the Lord and to hate evil (Proverbs 8:13).

Thus, we see why the father would tell his son to call wisdom his sister. Wisdom is characterized as more precious than silver and hidden treasure; she is a teacher of righteousness; she will be a blessing for those who possess her; her ways are pleasant and peaceful; she was used to create the world by the Lord, she keeps one from stumbling; she is a guardian; she is an exalter of those who possess her; and she will teach one to hate evil. Thus, we see why the father commands his son to say to wisdom, "You are my sister." The father wants the son to be loyal, love, and befriend wisdom as a sister because wisdom will lead his son into righteousness and away from evil and the adulterous woman (Proverbs 7:5).

We also see that the father commands the son to call insight his intimate friend. The word for *insight* comes from the original word *biynah*, which is also translated as understanding, knowledge, or insight. This word means more than just intellectual knowledge. It does include intellectual knowledge, but it is God-given knowledge to understand God's truth and to discern and apply these truths. The word for *intimate friend* comes from the original word *mowda,*` which can also mean kinsman. This is the only place where this word is used in the

Old Testament. This word is meant to invoke covenant loyalty to the son in that knowledge is to be called and treated as one having a shared identity and as a close relative. We also see that the verb *call* is written in the imperfect tense, which means that this is an incomplete action and implies that the son is to continue calling knowledge or insight his intimate friend.

Previously, we looked at how the son was to pursue a personal and intimate relationship with wisdom. In Hebrew literature, negative admonitions are also given, warning of the dangers of forsaking the father's wisdom. Thus, to not make wisdom one's intimate friend would be to treat wisdom as a stranger, a foreigner, an acquaintance, or an outsider. Throughout the book of Proverbs, we find admonitions and wise sayings such as these which warn of the danger and consequences of forsaking wisdom and not pursuing an intimate relationship with it:

- Fools despise wisdom and instruction (Proverbs 1:7).
- The father warns the son not to forsake his mother's teaching (Proverbs 1:8).
- Fools and the simple hate knowledge (Proverbs 1:22) and refuse to listen to knowledge (Proverbs 1:24–25).
- Turning away from knowledge is to hate knowledge and to shun the fear of the Lord (Proverbs 1:29).

- Fools who turn away from knowledge will be destroyed leading to utter disaster (Proverbs 1:32).
- Those who forsake wisdom walk in darkness, rejoice in evil, delight in perverseness, and are devious in their ways (Proverbs 2:13–15).

Therefore, we see why the father commands his son to call wisdom his sister and insight his intimate friend. Wisdom and knowledge will keep his son from sexual sin and the adulterous woman. However, to forsake, turn away, shun, or ignore wisdom is the path of the fool, the simple, the wicked, and the evil. To not pursue an intimate relationship with wisdom is to be a fool, despise wisdom, hate knowledge, be simple, not fear the Lord, bring destruction on oneself, walk in darkness, and delight in evil. The father's command to pursue a personal relationship with wisdom and knowledge is to protect him from the forbidden woman and the cunning deceptions of sexual sin and the adulteress.

The Father's Purpose for Instructing His Son on Sexual Sin

> *To keep you from the forbidden woman, from the adulteress with her smooth words.*
>
> —Proverbs 7:5

In the final verse of Proverbs 7 and after the father's nine commands, we are given the reason why the father gives these commands and why the father exhorts his son to obey them. These commands are meant to protect the son from the adulterous woman and sexual sin. In other words, the father's instruction is meant to act as a guardian, keeper, and protector from the adulterous woman.

The father does not want the son to be ignorant of her schemes and deceitful ways, so he has warned his son of her deceptive ways through his instruction. He has warned that the forbidden woman's lips drip honey (Proverbs 5:3). In the ancient world, honey was considered sweet, valuable, and satisfying. Figuratively, it can be used to describe the sweetness of God's Word (Proverbs 24:13) and as pleasant or nourishing words (Proverbs 16:24). Solomon also uses the image of honey being on the lips and under the tongue of his bride, which appears to suggest the anticipation of kissing one's bride, but it could also mean enjoying the pleasant sayings and speech of one's wife (Song of Solomon 4:11). We can surmise from Proverbs 5:3 that the father is warning the son that there is what appears to be sweetness, satisfaction and pleasantness in the adulteress's speech and even the excitement and anticipation of physical affection.

The father also warns that the adulteress has speech that is smoother than oil. This is simply warning that her speech is deceptive as she appears to provide nourishment, healing, and satisfaction. However, rather than possessing the nourishing and satisfying effects of honey, Proverbs 5:4 says, "*but in the end she is* ***bitter as wormwood****, sharp as a two-edged* *sword*" (emphasis added). Wormwood is intensely bitter and provides no satisfaction or nourishment. Additionally, in Deuteronomy 29:18 wormwood is used to describe a heart that turns away from the Lord to go and serve the gods of other nations where it says:

> *So that there will not be among you a man or woman, or family or tribe,* ***whose heart turns away today from the Lord our God, to go to serve the gods of those nations;*** *that there will not be among you a root bearing poisonous fruit and* ***wormwood*** (NASB, emphasis added).

Here, we can understand that the adulterous woman not only provides no spiritual satisfaction, but she also brings bitterness, sorrow, and turns one's heart away from God. Rather than receiving God's blessing, those that give in to the adulteress receive God's wrath (Proverbs 5:5–6).

The father also commands the son not to lust after the adulterous woman in his heart or be ensnared by her seductive actions (Proverbs 6:25). The father knows that the adulteress can and will use her beauty and her body as a means of temptation. She uses her physical attractiveness as temptation to turn an innocent glance into an enslaving lust that is cultivated in the heart. James warns of the progression of temptation to sin when he says, "*But each person is tempted when he is lured and enticed by his own desire. Then desire when it has conceived gives birth to sin, and sin when it is fully grown brings forth death*" (James 1:14–15). The adulteress will use her physical beauty and seductive manners to tempt, and this temptation is enticing (*deleazó*), and the enticement leads to lust or desire (*epithumia*), and lusting leads to sin (*hamartia*). This type of seduction and enticement is not new. The Lord was angry with the women of Jerusalem for this very sin in Isaiah 3:16 where he says the daughters of Zion are haughty, walk with outstretched necks, glancing wantonly with their eyes, mincing along as they go, and tinkling their feet. These actions were all meant to draw attention to themselves and had seductive and prideful intent. These provocative mannerisms were used to bring about temptation, lust, and sin.

This is the danger of sexual sin where thoughts can turn into sin. Ralph Waldo Emerson has said this regarding the devastating progression of sin, "Sow a thought and you reap an action; sow an act and you reap a habit; sow a habit and you reap a character; sow a character and you reap a destiny."[1] The adulteress is a master at enticing men to cultivate sin and lust in the heart, and as we know, lust leads to sin and sin to death. The sin of lusting in the heart is deadly, so the father wants to keep this temptation far away from his son.

Not only does the father warn of the adulterous woman's seductive behavior and deceptive speech to prevent the son from lusting for her in his heart, but he also instructs his son to stay far away from the adulteress and to not even go near her house (Proverbs 5:7–8). The father isn't advising the son to get close to the adulteress to see whether he can resist her seductive ways. No, he wants his son to stay away from her, so the son does not lust after her in his heart or be deceived by her empty, deceptive, and sinful lies that pierce like a sword rather than protect (Proverbs 5:4). This shows the father's great love for the son. He teaches about the adulterous woman and her deceptions to keep his son from sin. As we close this chapter, are we to believe that fathers and mothers are not to warn their sons and children of sexual sin? Are we to believe that it is too embarrassing or uncomfortable for a father to teach and instruct his son on this subject? Are we to believe that a father who has his son's best interest and loves his son is to bypass this instruction? Are we to believe that God the Father, God the Son, and God the Holy Spirit would advise fathers not to instruct and warn their sons of the dangers of sexual sin? May it never be!

Chapter 2

The Father Warns of the Consequences of Sexual Sins and Exhorts the Son Toward Purity

In chapter 1, we learned that it is the father's responsibility and duty to instruct his son about the dangers of sexual sin. In this chapter, we will reflect on Proverbs chapters 2, 5, and 6 where the father instructs the son by giving descriptive and factual statements, which profile the adulteress and sexual sin. The father also describes the consequences of giving into sexual sin and lust, and he exhorts his son as to how sexual intimacy is to be enjoyed in a God-pleasing way and how to avoid sexual sin. We will look closely at the father's descriptive and factual statements regarding the adulteress's seductive machinations, learn about the consequences of being seduced and led into her temptations, and end with the father's exhortation to enjoy sexual intimacy in the confines of marriage and avoid all other sexual sin and temptation.

Factual Descriptions of the Adulteress

The Adulteress Is Evil

The first thing we should learn about the adulteress is that she is wicked and evil. We learn this in Proverbs 6:24 where it says, "*to preserve you from the* ***evil*** *woman, from the smooth tongue of the adulteress*" (emphasis added). The father does not say the adulterous woman is misguided or a good person who has just lost her way. Not at all. The father calls the adulteress evil. The word *evil* comes from the original word *ra`* and is written as an adjective to describe the woman's character. The word *ra`* is used to describe that which embraces moral evil, wicked conduct, harmful intent, a malignant character, and the outworking of the evil behavior. The adulteress is not characterized as good, righteous, or God-fearing. She is evil, wicked, and God-hating. Likewise, sexual immorality and everything it entails is not good, righteous, or holy. It is not even neutral. The adulteress and sexual immorality are wicked and evil. The adulteress and sexual immorality are seen as that which God abhors because it is sinful and rebellious against what is good and pleasing to Him. The father wants the son to know that adultery and sexual immorality are evil and that God hates such behavior.

The Adulteress Uses Her Beauty and Seductive Mannerisms to Produce Lust in the Heart

The second thing we learn about the adulteress is that she uses her God-given physical beauty for evil rather than good. She uses her beauty and seductive mannerisms to produce lust in the heart. We see this in Proverbs 6:25 where it says, "*Do not desire her beauty in your heart, and do not let her capture you with her eyelashes.*" Beauty in and of itself is not sinful. However, the adulteress is skilled in using her physical appearance, seductive mannerisms, and gestures to seduce and entice her prey. It is not a sin to be beautiful; men and women are created in the image of God, and their bodies are created and fashioned by God in the womb (Genesis 1:26, Psalm 139:13–16). It is not wrong to dress in a way that accentuates one's God-given beauty, but it is quite another thing to dress, accentuate, and show off one's body in a provocative and seductive way to garner the attention of men or women with the intent to create lust in the heart.

When the father warns the son to not let the adulteress "*capture*" him with her eyelashes, he characterizes her seduction as that which seizes or captures a victim. In fact, in 1 Samuel 2:16, 1 Samuel 5:1, Joshua 11:19, the word *capture* is used to convey the idea of capturing land or an object. This is part and parcel with the adulteress and sexual sin. Today, we are bombarded with clothing designed to accentuate a woman's body and sexually suggestive advertising; there are pictures and videos on social media where women position their bodies in suggestive ways or utilize facial expressions to capture the attention of men and cultivate lust in the heart. Likewise, there are men who use these same techniques to seduce women. In either case, physical looks and suggestive mannerisms are the tool of the adulterer and adulteress; it is the method the world uses to seize and capture young men. The world's system floods the TV, internet, and social media with images and videos that are meant to entice and seduce. The father wants the son to be aware that both the adulteress and the world's system of sensuality are working to create lust in his heart and lead him into sin. The son is to be on his guard for these practices.

The Adulteress Uses Smooth and Deceptive Words

The adulteress uses deceptive words to lure her potential victims. We see this in Proverbs 2:16 where it says, "*So you will be delivered from the forbidden woman, from the adulteress with her* ***smooth words***" (emphasis added). The adulteress is dangerous because she's deceptive. Rather than speaking the truth, she conceals her true motives through deception. This is speech that has an end goal to manipulate, and it hides her true intentions. It's not that the adulteress is always outright lying, but she is skilled at twisting the truth. She is able to minimize sin with her twisted logic; she sneakily changes the meaning of love and turns it into lust. She can speak religious language to appear pious but is immoral and defiled.

Just as the adulterous woman sows her deceptive words, we see the same deceptive lies in today's society. We see unmarried couples reasoning that they need to live together to save money or see if they are compatible. We see men manipulate women by saying, "If you love me, you'll sleep with me." We see men who claim they've never committed physical adultery, but they deceive themselves by viewing internet filth and dirty magazines. We see men who justify that looking at pornography is better than committing adultery. We see unmarried professing Christians living together and justify this sinful act by saying, "Judge not lest ye be judged." We see this with pastors who put women in positions of power in the church so they can interact with them and form emotional relationships or counsel women and ask for intimate details that are explicit and completely inappropriate. We see this with men who seek vulnerable women and work under the guise of providing comfort when they really want to gratify their flesh. The deceptive speech of the adulterer or adulteress comes in many shapes and forms. The son is to be on his guard for deceptive speech, which sounds good or reasonable but inevitably leads to sin.

The Adulteress Is Unfaithful to Her Spouse and Has a Warped View of Sexual Sin

The adulteress is unfaithful to her spouse and to her marriage vows before God; she has an unbiblical view of her sexual sin. We see this in Proverbs 2:17 where it says, "*who forsakes the companion of her youth and forgets the covenant of her God.*" God's design for marriage is that there would be one man and one woman and that they would become husband and wife (Genesis 1:27, 2:23–24, Matthew 19:4–6, Ephesians 5:31). In fact, in Matthew 19:5 the Lord says this regarding how man and woman are to regard the commitment of marriage, "'*Therefore a man shall leave his father and his mother and* ***hold fast*** *to his wife, and the two shall become one flesh . . .*'" (emphasis added). The word for *hold fast* comes from the original word *kollaó,* which means to cling, to glue, or to cleave. This word pictures a strong soul-knit bond with a husband and wife clinging to one another physically, emotionally, and spiritually. In Matthew 19:5, the Lord says that the two shall become one flesh. This is a picture of covenant marriage and loyal, steadfast, faithful, volitional, and unconditional love between the man and woman. In God's plan for marriage, the husband and wife are to be fully committed and dedicated to one another. They are to fight, strive, and contend for unity and commitment to one another.

However, the biblical picture of marriage is foreign to the adulteress. She does not accept biblical teaching about the woman submitting to the husband as to the Lord (Ephesians 5:22); the husband acting as the head and leader of the wife and giving his life for his wife (Ephesians 5:23); the husband loving his wife self-sacrificially as Christ loved the church and gave Himself up for her (Ephesians 5:25); the husband teaching his wife Scripture and the Word of God and leading her in holiness (Ephesians 5:26–27); and the husband caring for, nourishing, and cherishing his wife's body as he would do the same for his own body (Ephesians 5:29, 33). The adulteress knows of no such submission or commitment to her husband. She spurns the husband's self-sacrificial love and exchanges it for lust. She is quick to forget her vows. She is swift to abandon and forsake her husband for the affection of other men. She esteems her marriage covenant as trivial. She does not walk before the Lord in humility or fear. She does not understand that her ways and thoughts are known and seen by the Lord (Proverbs 5:21). Rather than cling to her marriage, she severs her marriage. Sexual immorality has the effect of severing a marriage. Pornography and sexual immorality create distance rather than intimacy; they bring division and separation rather than fidelity and steadfastness. The son is to be on his guard for the woman who has a low view of sexual sin, low view of marriage, and a low view of God.

The Adulteress Uses Physical Touch and Appeals to the Lust of the Flesh

The adulteress appeals to the physical senses as we see in Proverbs 5:3 which says, "*For the* ***lips of a forbidden woman drip honey****, and her speech is smoother than oil*" (emphasis added). As we learned in chapter 1, the adulteress's lips drip honey, and this is most likely a reference to both deceptive speech and kisses. In fact, in the father's story, we learn that the adulteress uses kisses and physical touch to entice the young man (Proverbs 7:13). Thus, we can safely assume that the adulteress appeals to the physical touch and senses of her prey.

The adulterer or adulteress does not respect or honor physical boundaries. This is the person that seeks physical touch rather than protecting and preserving one's innocence. Whether this is in the context of a boyfriend-girlfriend relationship or a married spouse and an unmarried person, the adulterer or adulteress uses physical touch to appeal to the lust of the flesh (1 John 2:16, Galatians 5:19). This person is quick to initiate physical touch. They push physical boundaries, and they continue to press their victim with physical touch until the victim succumbs. They use physical touch under the guise of comfort when their true intention is seduction and temptation.

Women are to be on guard for men who push them to expose more of her body, who persists on pushing the boundaries of physical touch, and who openly share his past immoralities with little or no reservations. This is a man who is to be avoided. Men are to be aware of women who lack restraint and are overly physical in their touch. It is not to say that all forms of touching are sinful. However, it is to say that physical touch is a way to both show intimacy and affection as well as to seduce and entice. The son is to be on guard for the telltale sign of the woman who appeals to the lust of the flesh through physical touch or through physical senses in order to seduce and create lust in his heart that would cause him to succumb to sexual immorality.

The Adulteress Is an Unbeliever, Unrepentant, Wayward, and Ignorant of God

The adulteress is ignorant in spiritual matters and does not live a righteous or God-pleasing life; she does not know God. We see this in Proverbs 5:6 where it says, "*she does not* ***ponder the path of life****; her* ***ways wander****, and she* ***does not know it***" (emphasis added). Here, we see first see that she does not meditate, internalize, or value God's Word and instruction. In fact, the word for *ponder* comes from the original word *palac*, which conveys the idea of mentally weighing and pondering something. It is the picture of someone carefully assessing and evaluating something to discern godly morality. The adulteress is not concerned with carefully evaluating and understanding how the Word of God applies to all aspects of her life. As we mentioned earlier, she may use religious language, but she does not meditate and evaluate how God's Word is to direct her life. The adulteress does not write godly wisdom on the tablet of her heart or bind it on her fingers. Rather, she has a shallow knowledge of God's Word and godly wisdom. The adulteress may or may not use religious language, but from the father's story, we learn that she has only superficial knowledge of Scripture (Proverbs 7:14).

Additionally, the adulteress is marked by a wayward walk of life. The word for *wander* comes from the original word *nuwa`* and in this context, it conveys the idea of something being shaken and thus, wandering. It pictures instability rather than steadfastness. These are the characteristics that mark the adulteress; it is a lifestyle characterized by a lack of steadfastness and a walk of life that spiritually wanders. We see this same warning in the New Testament that unbelievers are characterized by a sinful and unrepentant walk of life. Paul gives this warning in 1 Corinthians 6:9–10 regarding the adulterers and sexually immoral:

> *Or do you not know that the unrighteous will not inherit the kingdom of God? Do not be deceived: neither the* ***sexually immoral****, nor idolaters, nor* ***adulterers****, nor* ***men who practice homosexuality****, nor thieves, nor the greedy, nor drunkards, nor revilers, nor swindlers will inherit the kingdom of God.* (emphasis added)

In Ephesians 5:5, Paul says the same thing regarding those who are marked by a sinful, wayward, and unrepentant walk of life where he says, "*For you may be sure of this, that everyone who is* ***sexually immoral or impure****, or who is covetous (that is an idolater), has no inheritance in the kingdom of Christ and God*" (emphasis added). Here, Paul states that those whose walk of life is marked by sexual immorality has no inheritance in the kingdom of Christ and God. Though they may claim to belong to Christ, their unrepentant walk of life that is characterized by sexual immorality demonstrates that they do not belong in Christ's kingdom. The Apostle John affirms the same thing regarding those who are marked by wayward and unrepentant walks of life in Revelation 21:8 where he says, "*But as for the cowardly, the faithless, the detestable, as for murderers,* ***the sexually immoral,*** *sorcerers, idolaters, and all liars, their portion will be in the lake that burns with fire and sulfur, which is the second death*" (emphasis added). The apostle John states that the unrepentant sexually immoral are those who will suffer forever in the lake of fire. Thus, we see that the adulteress is marked by a wayward and unrepentant life. She is an unbeliever, and she does not know God. The son is to be on guard for the telltale sign of the woman who has a superficial understanding of Scripture and is marked by a wayward and unrepentant walk of life.

Consequences of Giving into the Temptations of the Adulteress

Not only does the father instruct his son on how the adulteress tries to tempt and entice, but he also warns his son of the consequences of falling into sexual sin. In this section, we will progress from the physical consequences to the more devastating spiritual consequences.

Enslavement to Others and Monetary Loss

The first thing we learn is that sexual sin and adultery can have monetary consequences and cause a person to become enslaved to another. We see this in Proverbs 5:10 where it says, "*lest strangers take their fill of your strength, and your labors go to the house of a foreigner.*" We learned earlier that in the Old Testament, the punishment for adultery was death (Leviticus 20:10, Deuteronomy 22:22). However, even if the death sentence was not carried out, God still warns that there can be monetary consequences and enslavement. For example, in today's western society, divorce as a result of adultery or having children outside of marriage, can result in significant child and/or alimony payments. The person who ends up paying these costs becomes monetarily enslaved to the ex-wife, ex-husband, or ex-partner. These payments can be temporary, permanent, or large lump-sum payments.

Proverbs 6:26 says that the adulteress reduces and strips men of everything valuable such as honor, wealth, and spiritual well-being: "*For the price of a prostitute reduces one to a loaf of bread, and an adulteress hunts for a precious life*" (NASB). Here, the adulteress is pictured as one who diminishes her victims. She does not provide satisfaction and spiritual well-being; rather she robs, steals, and enslaves. When it says she reduces men to a loaf of bread, this may speak of the loss of a good name and honor, but it appears that it could also strongly imply monetary losses because to be reduced to a loaf of bread implies that someone has been reduced to something that is inexpensive. Thus, those falling into sexual sin and adultery can become slaves to others and forfeit their labor, money, and strength.

Dishonor and Disgrace

Committing sexual sin and adultery can lead to the loss of a good name, reputation, and honor. We see this in Proverbs 6:33 where it says, "*He will get wounds and **dishonor**, and* *his* ***disgrace*** *will not be wiped away"* (emphasis added). The word for *dishonor* comes from *qalown*, which conveys a state of public dishonor, reproach, and humiliation as a result of violating God's commands. This is more than inward guilt; it represents visible disgrace. Thus, what is done in secret and in hidden rooms ends up becoming public shame and leads to dishonor and reproach. There can be dishonor on many levels as it relates to sexual sin and adultery. Dishonor may result in the loss of a job because a deviant relationship was uncovered in the workplace, and the adulterer loses the trust of the company for secretive and untrustworthy behavior. Dishonor may come from the adulterer's children who revolt and no longer trust, revere, or respect them. Rather, they may scorn and disrespect their parent for betraying the other parent and the family. Dishonor may come in the church for a pastor, elder, deacon, or church member who is caught in adultery, viewing pornography, being flirtatious and unguarded in their speech; they may lose the trust, honor, and respect of the church (Proverbs 5:14). Sexual sin and adultery lead to dishonor.

Once exposed, sexual sin brings disgrace and shame in Proverbs 6:33. The word for *disgrace* comes from the original word *cherpah* and means reproach, scorn, or contempt. Once again, this word conveys public shame and contempt for disobedient behavior before God and men. This word signals a rupture in a relationship with God, which exposes the offender to shame. The adulterer or adulteress have the stain and reproach of being unfaithful to their covenant before God. Additionally, there is also the public disgrace and shame that accompanies sexual sin and adultery. For example, a congregation or community may ask the following questions:

- How long was this person committing adultery?
- How many people has this person committed adultery with?
- Is this person also involved in viewing pornography, and if so, are we now concerned that he may need to be investigated by authorities?
- What kind of lies and manipulation did this person use to cover up their sin?
- Did anyone else know about this behavior and help this person cover it up?
- Who has this person lied to and do the lies extend to work, family, and friends?

These are only but a few questions that a congregation or community may ask. As we see, these questions stir up even greater shame and dishonor as the congregation or community sees the individual as not just an adulterer, but also as a liar, manipulator, pervert, deceiver, and more. We see dishonor when pastors are exposed and shown to be in adulterous relationships in the church; they bring dishonor to God and dishonor to the church. We see this when a husband and wife are divorced, and this results in a broken home and wayward children. Sexual sin does not result in the father or mother being honored, but rather, it leads to sin, dishonor, disgrace, and other devastating results. The father desires that the son live a God-fearing life, and he warns his son of the consequences of committing sexual sin because those who commit such sins face hardship and a loss of honor. The father states this again in Proverbs 5:9, "*lest you give your **honor** to others and your years to the merciless*" (emphasis added). To commit adultery and sexual sin is to give away one's honor in exchange for disgrace, reproach, and shame.

Physical Consequences and Disease

Committing sexual sin and adultery can result in regret and venereal diseases that ravage the body. We see this in Proverbs 5:11 which says, "*and at the end of your life you groan, when **your flesh and body are consumed***" (emphasis added). We learned earlier that the adulterer will potentially lose their material wealth and be enslaved to others, but here we learn that there may also be serious physical consequences for sexual sin. The word for "consumed" comes from *kalah*, and in this context, it conveys the idea of being spent, wasting away, or brought to an end.

In Proverbs 5:11, it could mean that one's body and flesh are consumed, exhausted, and spent from years of giving their life away and giving their labor to others. However, this could also refer to physical consequences that could result from sexual sin. This could include devastating and deadly sexually transmitted diseases such as HIV, syphilis, or Hepatitis B. It might also include devastating sexually transmitted diseases such as chlamydia, gonorrhea, herpes, or other diseases that can be painful and potentially even passed onto infants if the mother is infected and passes on the disease to the infant. In the ancient world, the use of medicine to treat bacterial infections was non-existent. There were no antiviral medications either. Thus, the one contracting the disease was left to suffer.

The Apostle Paul seems to refer to this consequence in 1 Corinthians 5:5 when he says this regarding the case of incest in the Corinthian church: "*You are to deliver this man to Satan for the* ***destruction of the flesh****, so that his spirit may be saved in the day of the Lord*" (emphasis added). Here we see that Paul desires that the man who is committing incest be saved because he says that he desires that "*his spirit may be saved in the day of the Lord.*" However, the man will reap destruction to his flesh for indulging in this immorality. Paul seems to be suggesting that there could be physical consequences for engaging in such immoral behavior, so it's not unreasonable to assume that Proverbs 5:5 could refer to the possibility of physical disease as a consequence of sexual sin and adultery. The physical pain, the risk of potential death, and the risk of contracting or passing on venereal disease to another person should serve as a dire warning against indulging in sexual sin and adultery. The father does not want this for his son, so he warns him of this devastating consequence.

The Wrath of the Adulteress's Husband

Another consequence is that committing adultery will stir up the unmerciful wrath of the adulteress's husband. We see this in Proverbs 6:27–29 and 33–35:

> *Can a man carry fire next to his chest and his clothes not be burned? Or can one walk on hot coals and his feet not be scorched? So is he who goes in to his neighbor's wife; none who touches her will go unpunished. . . . He will get wounds and dishonor, and his disgrace will not be wiped away. For jealousy makes a man furious, and he will not spare when he takes revenge. He will accept no compensation; he will refuse though you multiply gifts.*

From these verses, we learn of the merciless wrath that the husband of the adulteress may take out on the man who committed adultery with his wife. In Proverbs 6:27–28, the father warns the son and provides two analogies to demonstrate the inevitable consequences of sexual sin.

The first analogy is that it is impossible to carry fire next to your chest and not be burned. This is a warning that sexual sin always carries consequences, and you cannot commit such sin without bearing consequences just as it's impossible to carry fire without being burned. These consequences may occur immediately, or they may come later. The father provides a second analogy for the son, saying that it is impossible to walk on hot coals and not be scorched. This analogy is used to warn his son that it is impossible to indulge in sexual sin without consequences. Consider this story told by John Macarthur after speaking with a couple who shared about the unintended and unforeseen consequences of indulging in a life of immorality:

> I remember some years ago talking to a young couple who had lived sinful lives, lives of fornication, sexual indulgence before they were saved, and came to Christ and then married, became believers. And I remember talking to the husband. I said, "How are you getting along? How's it going?" He said, "It's really hard." I said, "Why?" [He said] "I have too many memories of too many sins with too many other women."[2]

Consider another story that John Macarthur shared about a member at Grace Community Church who regretted his past sins and struggled with the consequences of his past immoral actions:

> I remember baptizing a man at Grace Church who was a homosexual and the Lord wonderfully saved him. His life was changed and he moved into a new circle of friends and he removed himself as far as possible from his former lifestyle, but he admitted to me that the hardest thing he had to face was his own mind retracing all those immoral experiences, and they were many for many, many years. He had indulged himself with so many vile behaviors that he

> found the struggle was almost unbearable to wash them out of his mind.[3]

This is the kind of consequence the father is warning his son about. Even if the person thinks they have escaped physical punishment and the wrath of a vengeful spouse, they will still bear spiritual scars and memories that do damage. They cannot carry fire without being burned, and they cannot walk on hot coals without bearing burn marks.

In Proverbs 6:29, he reemphasizes that any man who commits adultery will be punished and in Proverbs 6:31, the father says that if the person is caught, he will pay sevenfold and give all the goods of his house away. Stating that the person will pay sevenfold conveys the idea of full and severe discipline. In fact, the term *sevenfold* is used this way in Genesis 4:15 and in Leviticus 26:27–28. It is a picture of unmitigated, unrestrained, and unquenched vengeance. This is the full unbridled and unquenched wrath that a husband or spouse may seek to take out on the adulterer or adulteress.

In Proverbs 6:33–35, the father warns that those who commit adultery or sexual sin only receive dishonor and wounds. The word for wounds in Proverbs 6:33 comes from the original word *nega`* and can mean infection, plague, affliction, stripe, blow, or sore. In this context, the term most likely refers to physical retaliation since it is the adulteress's husband who delivers the wounds. In either case, the adulterer does not receive satisfaction, but rather, wounds. Additionally, in Proverbs 6:34–35, the father tells the son that the adulteress's husband will be furious, show no mercy, and accept no bribe or compensation for what the adulterer did with his wife. This is a severe warning that the husband of the adulterer cannot be bribed with money or begged for mercy. Rather, the picture is of a wrathful husband that will ruthlessly take his revenge using any means possible to ensure that the man who committed adultery with his wife is punished to the greatest extent possible. Even today, we hear of instances where angry spouses murder the adulterer and the unfaithful spouse in unforgiving fury; furious spouses will take any means possible to destroy the reputation of the adulterer by publicly exposing their actions. The father is emphasizing that there is nothing to turn away the wrath of the adulteress's husband; though the adulterer will desire mercy, they must expect wrath. The adulterer might try to compensate the husband with money, gifts, and bribes, but they must expect stripes and blows. Though the adulterer would desire secrecy so their reputation is kept intact, they must expect public shame, dishonor, and disgrace.

Bondage to Sin and the Destruction of One's Soul

Committing adultery or sexual sin can lead to bondage to sin and the destruction of one's soul. Sexual sin has a devastating effect in that it keeps the person in bondage to the sin as Proverbs 5:22 explains: "*The iniquities of the wicked* ***ensnare*** *him, and he is* ***held fast*** *in the cords of his sin*" (emphasis added). The word *ensnare* comes from the original word *lakad*, which conveys the picture of being caught or captured in a net or a trap and being ensnared. The father warns that committing sexual sin can entangle and twist someone to the point that they cannot get out. It is a picture of someone being caught in a trap and unable to free themselves from a trap. The statement by Ralph Waldo Emerson cited earlier is apropos: thoughts lead to actions, actions lead to habits, habits lead a character, and a character leads to a destination. Sexual sin is dangerous in that it is enticing, promises fulfillment, traps its victims, and keeps them in bondage. It is not a harmless or innocent sin. No, it is a sin that captures, entangles, twists, and leaves one in bondage. It is not a small thing to day-dream of sexual encounters, look at pornography, fornicate, or commit adultery. No, it is an enticing trap of the devil used to keep men in bondage to sexual sin.

Much is written about widespread use of pornography in today's society. However, what the world does not understand is that this is not pornography addiction. Rather, it is enslavement to sin and unrighteousness (Romans 6:16). The spiritual condition of so-called believers who are caught, ensnared, and enslaved to sexual sin indicates that they may be people who made a false profession of faith and are unregenerate. Although true Christians fall into sin, let's give Proverbs 5:22 its due weight and encourage those who are ensnared in any kind of sexual sin to examine whether they are in the faith (2 Corinthians 13:5). From what we read in Scripture, it is very likely that those who are trapped and ensnared in sexual sin do not know the Lord and are unregenerate; if so, the wrath of God abides on them.

Additionally, we see that sexual sin not only keeps people in bondage, but it destroys their soul and can lead to spiritual death. We see this in Proverbs 6:32, which says, "*He who commits adultery lacks sense; he who does it destroys himself.*" So not only can sexual sin keep someone in bondage, but it can also reveal that the person who unrepentantly commits these sins lacks wisdom and that they are destroying themselves. Those who commit unrepentant sexual sin are literally killing their soul. Unrepentant sexual sin is not the way of life; it is the way of spiritual death (Proverbs 2:17–19); it is a two-edged sword that kills the soul (Proverbs 5:4–5). These are the consequences that accompany sexual sin. What would it profit a man if he indulged in every adulterous relationship presented to him, indulged in every lustful thought, and viewed every sexually immoral type of media that he could consume yet forfeited, destroyed, and damned his own soul (Matthew 16:26)? The inevitable answer is that he would not profit, but would suffer the loss of his soul to eternal damnation. The father wants his son to be aware of the physical and spiritual consequences of committing this sin. This is the father's warning and rebuke to keep his son far away from sexual sin so that he does not destroy his body or his soul.

The Father's Exhortation on Avoiding Sexual Sin and the Adulteress

Not only does the father instruct his son on how the adulteress will tempt him but he also describes the consequences of committing sexual sin and exhorts his son on how sexual intimacy is to be enjoyed in a God-pleasing way. The father's instruction includes teaching, reproof, correction, and training in righteousness (2 Timothy 3:16). He not only states what needs to be avoided, but he also positively exhorts his son to walk in a way that pleases the Lord. In this section, we will review the father's exhortation on how to avoid sexual sin and enjoy physical intimacy in the confines of marriage.

Abstain and Flee from Sexual Immorality

In Proverbs 5:8 the father commands his son to stay far away from the adulteress: "***Keep your way far from her***, *and* ***do not go near the door of her house***" (emphasis added). The word *keep* is written in the imperative, which means this is a command. The son is not to see how close he can get to sexual sin and resist temptation. No! The son is to stay far away from sexual sin and the adulteress. In fact, the original word for keep comes from *rachaq*, which conveys the idea of deliberate separation or relational estrangement. The son is to stay far away from sexual sin and avoid temptation. In Proverbs 5:8 the father commands the son not to even go near the adulteress's house. The idea behind both commands is to stay far away and never come close to sexual sin to protect against temptation. John Macarthur has helpful wisdom about staying far away from sexual sin:

> Stay away from sexual sin. Now young people always want to say, "How far away? How far away do I have

to stay?" Which means, "How far can I go and still be okay?" "Is it okay, you know, to hold hands and hug each other? Is it okay to kiss? Is it okay to touch each other? Is it okay to go beyond that as long as you don't do the very act? What can I do? Is it okay if we're engaged? Is it okay if we've decided that we're really the ones and somewhere down the road we are going to get married? How far can I go?"

That isn't even the right question. That question betrays a sinful heart. The question isn't how far can I go and get away with it? The question is, how can I be sanctified, separated from sin, and holy unto God? That's the question. That's the question. How can I conduct my physical relationships so that I am holy, which means separated from sin? And as you begin to play with the emotions that God has designed to lead to consummation and intercourse, you begin to allow your mind to move into the area of thinking about that, you are in sin because if a man's mind commits adultery, in God's eyes he's committed it, right? If a woman commits it in the mind, it's been committed before God because He sees the mind.

You have to stop short of the impure thought, the impure motive, the lustful passion.[4]

This is what the father is commanding the son. The father wants his son to be separated from sin. The father doesn't want the son to be exposed to, tempted by, or enticed by sexual sin. The father commands the son that he is to keep far away from sin and never go near it.

The Apostle Paul gives a similar command to the Thessalonians about staying far away from sexual sin: "*For this is the will of God, your sanctification: that you* ***abstain*** *from* ***sexual immorality***" (1 Thessalonians 4:3, emphasis added). Here, we see that God's desire for the believer's sanctification is to abstain from sexual immorality. The word for abstain is written in the present tense and infinitive mood, which simply means that this is to be the habitual practice of the believer. Additionally, the word *abstain* conveys the idea of being distant and separating from something. The word for sexual immorality comes from the word *porneia*, which is also translated as fornication, immorality, or sexual immorality. This word is used broadly to describe the selling off of sexual purity for any type of sexual impurity. This could include sex outside of marriage, pornography, lustful thoughts, lustful actions and self-gratification, including incest, and every type of sexually impure thought, word, deed, or intent. Paul simply restates what the father commands in Proverbs 5:8, which is to stay far away and abstain from sexual immorality of all types. It is the will of God that believers abstain from sexual immorality, and it is the will of God that fathers instruct their sons to abstain from every thought, word, deed, or intent that is sexually immoral.

Not only are we to stay far away from anything sexually immoral, but we are also commanded to flee from it. In Paul's first letter to the Corinthians, he gives them this command regarding the necessity to flee from sexual sin in 1 Corinthians 6:18: "***Flee from sexual immorality***. *Every other sin a person commits is outside the body, but the sexually immoral person sins against his own body*" (emphasis added). The word *flee* comes from the original word *pheugó,* which means to escape or run away from. Paul writes this command in the present tense and imperative mood, which simply means that this is a command to continually be obeyed. Additionally, the word *pheugó* conveys the idea of taking flight and escaping a thing or situation. This word does not give the idea of just casually turning and walking the other way. This word conveys the idea of running away, fleeing, and escaping for one's life. Zac Poonen gives a helpful statement as it relates to fleeing from sexual sin:

> Flee from immorality! Flee when you see a pornographic book! What should you do? Turn around and run for your life! You accidentally came across a pornographic site on the computer? Get up from your chair and run for your life or switch out the computer immediately, or close the page! For your life! Don't just gently [say] "Oh, what should I do now?" Then you haven't understood how serious

> immorality is. That's a weak attitude toward sin with a lot of believers; particularly sexual sin. And that's why the devil just laughs at them. The devil messes up their house, and they can't do anything.
>
> "What to do brother? The devil's come and messed up my house." I'll tell you why he's messed up your house, you don't run away from sin. That's why he doesn't run away from you. He says, "Who are you? I know Jesus and Paul but who are you? I know the attitude Jesus and Paul had toward sin and I know your attitude also. Who are you? You think you can fight me? Ha, you and I are on the same side," he says. He who has ears to hear, let him hear. Flee from immorality, and Satan will flee from you. He doesn't say stand there and fight it. No! . . . As soon as you see some flirtatious girl, [or] maybe someone in the church avoid her![5]

Paul says it a different way in Ephesians 5:3 when he is speaking of being imitators of Christ and not being associated with sexual immorality where he says, "*But* ***sexual immorality*** *and all impurity or covetousness* ***must not even be named among you,*** *as is proper among saints*" (emphasis added). Paul is commanding that sexual immorality not to be named among the Ephesian believers. The word *named* is written in the present tense and imperative mood, which simply means that this is a command to continually be followed. Paul is stating that sexual immorality should not be named, mentioned with, or associated with the people of God. The people of God should not be indulging in, committing, or associated with anything related to sexual immorality. This includes pornography, men and women living together and fornicating before marriage, being sexually provocative and tempting others to sin, and any other sexually immoral behavior. This type of sin is not proper among the saints. Not only is it not proper, but Paul also says that those that live like this have no inheritance in the kingdom of Christ and God (Ephesians 5:5). The saints are called to a holy life, not unrestrained immorality (2 Timothy 1:9). The father desires that his son abstain from, flee from, and not be associated with sexual immorality. When the son sees sexual sin and temptation, he is to turn around and flee for his life and not be associated with it. He is not to give it a base of operation. He is not to allow it to form a beachhead where he can be attacked and tempted. No, he is to abstain and flee from sexual sin!

Deal Radically and Repentantly with Sexual Sin

The father wisely commands his son to deal radically with sexual sin. In Proverbs 6:25 he says, "*Do not desire her beauty in your heart, and do not let her capture you with her eyelashes.*" In this short verse, he gives the son two commands—to not lust for the adulteress's beauty in his heart and to not be carried away by her seductive manners, provocative gestures, or alluring physical features. It is a warning and command from the father to abstain from sexual immorality, not let sexual thoughts and lust begin in either the mind or the heart, and to be aware and deal with the formation and cultivation of sexual lust in the heart.

Great men of God have commented on the need to kill and deal radically with sin throughout church history. Below are some insightful comments and exhortations on the Christian's responsibility to abstain from, repent of, fight, and kill sin in one's life:

- "We seek to throttle sin and crush it from our lives, sapping it of its strength, rooting it out, and depriving it of its influence. That is what it means to mortify sin." [6]
- "Do you mortify [sin]; do you make it your daily work; be always at it whilst you live; cease not a day from this work; be killing sin or it will be killing you." [7]
- "Do you want to put to death the lusts in your heart? Then stop entertaining them. Peter does not prescribe a program of therapy. He does not suggest that such sin be treated as an addiction. He simply says to abstain. Quit doing it. You have no business indulging such thoughts. Put them away at once. You yourself must do this; it cannot be done for you. There is no point waiting for

some heavenly power to erase this sin automatically from your life. You are to stop it, and stop it immediately."[8]

- "Sin is not mortified when it is merely covered up. . . . You have not done your duty regarding your sin until you have confessed and forsaken it."[9]
- "Sin is not mortified when it is only internalized. If you forsake the outward practice of some evil yet continue to ruminate on the memory of that sin's pleasures, beware. You may have moved your sin into the privacy of your imagination, where it is known only to you and to God, but that sin has not been mortified. If anything, it has been made more deadly by being married to pretended righteousness."[10]
- "Sin is not mortified when it is exchanged for another sin."[11]
- "Sin is not mortified when it is merely repressed."[12]
- "Pull it out, look at it, denounce it, hate it for what it is; then you have really dealt with it. You must not merely push it back in a spirit of fear, and in a timorous manner. Bring it out, expose it, and analyze it; and then denounce it for what it is until you hate it."[13]

- "We should deal with our sin courageously, striking at its head. Subduing it a little bit is not enough. We need to exterminate it, hack it in pieces-seek by the means of grace and the power of the Spirit to wring the deadly life from it."[14]

The father commands his son not to lust in his heart; this is exactly what Jesus was speaking of in Matthew 5:28–30 where he said:

> *But I say to you that* ***everyone who looks at a woman with lustful intent has already committed adultery with her in his heart****. If your right eye causes you to sin, tear it out and throw it away. For it is better that you lose one of your members than that your whole body be thrown into hell. And if your right hand causes you to sin, cut it off and throw it away. For it is better that you lose one of your members than that your whole body go into hell* (emphasis added).

Sexual immorality and all sin come from the heart (Matthew 5:19). Jesus proclaimed that lustful thoughts in the heart are sinful and that just one lustful intent in the heart was enough to send someone to hell. Therefore, Jesus exhorted mankind to deal radically with sin. He commanded that mankind act radically to kill and forsake their own personal sin. The radical repentance that Jesus calls for is not physical mutilation, but rather, spiritual amputation.

Biblical repentance is frequently characterized as a violent act:

- Jesus describes the kingdom of heaven being taken by violence, and the violent claiming it (Matthew 11:12). Biblical repentance isn't passive. Rather, it is characterized as forcefully, violently, and zealously repenting unto salvation in Jesus Christ.
- Paul speaks of the violence of entering the kingdom of heaven when he says that those who belong to Christ Jesus have crucified the flesh with is passions and desires (Galatians 5:24). This pictures an individual nailing their own sinful desires and old sinful man to a cross and killing it. Thus, repentance is characterized as purposefully and intentionally killing one's old self and sinful desires (Ephesians 4:22).
- Jesus pictures repentance as the gouging out of eyes and the cutting off of hands (Matthew 5:29–30); He describes repentance as denying yourself and refusing to associate with your sinful desires, self-righteousness, and self-will (Matthew 16:24). There are many who rub their eyes and scratch their hands when dealing with sin, but the Lord of heaven pictures true repentance as the purposeful act of gouging out body parts and cutting off of limbs as a radical and violent way of dealing with sin in one's life.

- Paul speaks of the violent nature of the Christian putting to death the deeds of the body and sin by the power of the Holy Spirit (Romans 8:13). Paul does not speak of sin as something to nourish or cherish. Rather, he speaks of killing sin in one's life. It is the picture of taking sin in one's life and killing it by any means necessary such as strangling, impaling, drowning, or starving.
- Paul speaks of the violent nature of starving and killing sin by making no provision for the flesh to gratify its desires (Romans 13:14). In 2 Corinthians 7:11, he pictures true repentance as an eagerness to turn from sin, having holy indignation and anger with your personal sin, having fear of bringing shame to God's name and God's glory, longing for godliness, and having zeal for holiness (2 Corinthians 7:11).

Therefore, we see how Jesus and Paul speak of the violent and zealous nature of repentance in which an individual is radical in dealing with their own sin. The individual who has true repentance is pictured as taking the sin in their life and starving it to death, maiming it, and violently killing it. True repentance pictures an individual deliberately shunning and refusing to associate with their sin. Moreover, true repentance pictures the violent and aggressive attitude of killing, starving, maiming, denying, shunning, and turning from sin in one's life and a continual turning to Christ. This is exactly what the father is commanding his son to do—to deal radically with sin. The son is not to cultivate lustful thoughts or entertain sexual sins in the heart. The son is to forsake, turn away from, flee from, repent of, violently kill, maim, crucify, and destroy lustful and sexual sins which take place and form in the heart. These are the father's exhortations to abstain from, flee from, and radically repent of sexual sin. His instructions are in complete agreement with what we see in the New Testament.

Enjoy Intimacy in Marriage

The father exhorts his son to enjoy sexual intimacy in the confines of marriage. We see this in Proverbs 5:18–19 where he says to his son, "*Let your fountain be blessed, and* ***rejoice in the wife of your youth****, a lovely deer, a graceful doe.* ***Let her breasts fill you at all times with delight; be intoxicated always in her love***" (emphasis added). In contrast with the adulteress who is bitter as wormwood, destructive as a sharp two-edged sword, and on the path to death (Proverbs 5:4–6), the faithful wife is characterized as a fountain of blessing.

Many points that we see in Proverbs 5:18–19 are worth noting. We see that the Lord blesses a marriage between one man and one wife, and that this is His design for marriage. We also see that the wife is characterized as a continually flowing fountain that will be a source of blessing and fulfillment; she is to be the source of the husband's sexual satisfaction in marriage. Rather than wormwood, she is a beautiful animal, a graceful doe; the wife's body and physical affection are to be the husband's satisfaction at all times, and he is to delight in her. This does not mean that the husband and wife give their whole life toward physical intimacy, but rather, that the husband and wife can enjoy physical intimacy at any time in their marriage. It means there are no bounds or limits to the affection that can be shared between a husband and a wife. The husband does not need to go elsewhere to find satisfaction because satisfaction is found between him and his wife.

Additionally, we see that the husband is to be intoxicated with his wife's love. The word for intoxicated comes from the original word *shagah*, which means to be enraptured with. This word can have negative connotation but, in this context, it is positive. Physical intimacy between a man and a woman in marriage is not pictured as something that should be enjoyed scarcely or with great caution. Rather, the physical intimacy in marriage is viewed as something that should be greatly and abundantly enjoyed. The husband and the wife are to be enraptured with one another and greatly enjoy this aspect of marriage.

We also see that this physical intimacy is a form and expression of love in a marriage. We see this when the father tells his son to be intoxicated or enraptured in her love. Please note that the father does not call this lust nor does he does not call this sexual immorality. No, he calls this physical intimacy between a man and a woman in marriage "love." Anything outside the marriage would be considered lust, but within the confines of marriage, physical intimacy is called "love" by King Solomon, God the Father, God the Son, and God the Holy Spirit. Paul affirms that physical intimacy in marriage is to be enjoyed as well:

> *But because of the temptation to sexual immorality, each man should have his own wife and each woman her own husband.* ***The husband should give to his wife her conjugal rights, and likewise the wife to her husband****. For the wife does not have authority over her own body, but the husband does. Likewise the husband does not have authority over his own body, but the wife does.* ***Do not deprive one another, except perhaps by agreement for a limited time, that you may devote yourselves to prayer****; but then come together again, so that Satan may not tempt you because of your lack of self-control.*
>
> —1 Corinthians 7:2–5 emphasis added

In these verses, Paul affirms that the husband and wife are one flesh and that they are to enjoy physical intimacy with one another, freely give themselves to one another and not depriving one another of this physical intimacy without good cause.

The father describes the wife as "*the wife of your youth,*" which simply speaks of her as the woman that the man married when he was young. It implies faithfulness and loyalty to the wife regardless of her age. The Bible speaks at length about covenant faithfulness and the biblical duties of the husband. This includes the husband being the head, leader, and savior of the wife (Ephesians 5:23). The husband is not the savior of his wife because we know that Christ is the only Savior of the world. However, the husband mimics Christ in that he gives of himself to nurture her in Scripture, protect her, and lead her in truth. This is what it means that the husband is to act as a savior; he is not and never can be the true Savior because only Christ fulfills that role. The husband is to self-sacrificially love his wife as Christ loved the church and gave himself up for the church (Ephesians 5:25). This is a picture of self-sacrificial love that seeks what is best for the wife. The husband is to lead, teach, and instruct his wife in Scripture (Ephesians 5:26). The husband is not to be ignorant, apathetic, or unknowledgeable in Scripture. Rather, he is to be one who sanctifies his wife through instruction and care in the Word of God (Ephesians 5:27). The husband is to care for his wife's body as he would care for his own body (Ephesians 5:29). He is to hold fast to his wife in marriage and do everything within his ability to stay united with his wife as one flesh (Ephesians 5:31). The husband is to love his wife as himself, which simply means that he must diligently watch over and care for his wife and not treat her less than he would treat his own body (Ephesians 5:33). Thus, the Bible pictures the husband as a lover, protector, guide, sanctifier, preserver, caregiver, companion, leader, and savior of his wife. The husband is to enjoy the wife of his youth, enjoy physical intimacy with his wife, protect her, guide her, bring her up in the Word, self-sacrificially love her, stay united with her, and care for and enjoy the wife of his youth.

The father also talks about covenant fidelity and loyalty in Proverbs 5:15: "*Drink water from your own cistern, flowing water from your own well.*" The son is not to look for a woman other than his wife to satisfy all his sexual needs, wants, or desires. Rather, he is to enjoy physical intimacy only with his wife. Once again, the father pictures the wife as flowing water from a well, which describes the abundant satisfaction and fulfillment that is to be had between a husband and a wife.

Finally, the author of the book of Hebrews make this statement about honoring marriage in a God-pleasing way: "*Let marriage be held in honor among all, and let the marriage bed be undefiled, for God will judge the sexually immoral and adulterous*" (Hebrews 13:4). Sexual intimacy and marriage are honored when physical intimacy is between a husband and a wife. Homosexual marriage and activity, unmarried men and women living together, pornography, adultery, self-gratification, or any other sexually immoral thought, word, deed, or intent is not God-honoring. The New Testament writers are extremely clear that those who live unrepentant sexually immoral lives do not know God (1 Thessalonians 4:5), disregard the Lord's call to holiness (1 Thessalonians 4:7), disregard God (1 Thessalonians 4:8), are deceived and will not inherit the kingdom of God (1 Corinthians 6:9, Ephesians 5:5), will receive the wrath of God and are sons of disobedience (Ephesians 5:6), are in darkness (Ephesians 5:8), will be judged (Hebrews 13:4), and will be thrown in the lake that burns with fire and sulfur (Revelation 21:8). Marriage is to be honored, and the father diligently seeks to instruct his son on how to honor God by honoring God's plan for marriage. The father is continually instructing his son on how the world views marriage and sexuality versus how God views marriage and sexuality:

- The world applauds divorce, but God desires dedication.
- The world encourages promiscuity, but God desires purity.
- The world advocates homosexual marriage, but God desires heterosexual marriage.
- The world promotes immorality and infidelity, but God desires fidelity.
- The world favors lust, but God desires love.
- The world champions sin, but God desires sanctification.

As we close this chapter, we see that the Christian father is a wise and godly man. The father describes who the adulteress is and how she deceives, and he warns the son what happens to those who give into sexual sin. The father explains how to avoid sexual sin and exhorts his son to pursue holiness and enjoy physical intimacy with his wife and in the confines of marriage. The biblical father is one who teaches his son how to live a God-pleasing life in matters of sexuality and physical intimacy.

Chapter 3

The Father's Story: The Adulterous Predator and the Death of the Foolish Young Man

As we transition into this chapter, there is a magnificent break in the flow of Proverbs 7 that occurs at verse 6. The father transitions from commanding his son to listen and obey his teaching to telling a story of a young man who lacked wisdom, knowledge, and insight regarding the adulteress and sexual sin.

This is a brilliant story that the Holy Spirit inspired Solomon to write. He tells of the devastation of young men who lack wisdom, the religious façade and deceptive lies of the adulteress, the machinations the adulteress uses to appeal to the flesh, the vivid imagery of a predator stalking its prey, and the outwitted prey being led to the slaughter. This story details how temptation leads to enticement, enticement leads to lust, lust leads to sin, and sin leads to death (James 1:14–15). This story is masterful in that it provides specific detail, yet it leaves out explicit, perverse, and graphic detail to preserve the son's conscience. It is a marvelously instructive story inspired by God illustrating how fathers are to teach their sons. The groundwork we have laid in the first two chapters will pay dividends in helping you understand how the wiles and deceptions of the adulteress and sexual sin can deceive and kill those lacking godly wisdom.

We will do a verse-by-verse exposition of the father's story in Proverbs 7:6–23. As I exposit this text, I am going to make several points in an ordinal series (e.g., first, second, third, fourth, etc.). It's not that the points rank higher or lower than others, but rather, it is intended to help the reader understand the important themes and wisdom that are masterfully crafted into the story. Let's begin our exposition.

> *For at the window of my house I have looked out through my lattice, and I have seen among the simple, I have perceived among the youths, a young man lacking sense.*
>
> —Proverbs 7:6–7

As the father begins his story, he speaks from the perspective of an event that occurred in the past. This is a real-life account of an event where the adulteress applied her deception, and a young man was caught. Storytelling is a powerful teaching method that makes the father's instructions tangible and applicable.

So first, notice that the father is wise in how he teaches his son. All fathers could learn a lesson from this father. Fathers can use real life past or present events to demonstrate lessons to their sons. In this case, the father uses a past event in which a young man without godly wisdom is tempted by the adulteress. The father is purposeful in recalling this past event because he wants the son to realize that this event happened to a young man, and it could happen to his son. Fathers can and should use past and present events to teach their sons. Whether these events include pastors falling into adultery, presidents falling into adultery, men falling into adultery in the workplace, young men living with their girlfriend outside of marriage, men succumbing to and being enslaved to pornography, or any other event that involves immorality, the father can use these events to teach his son. Utilizing stories and analyzing present-day events is a powerful way to make the father's instruction tangible.

Second, let's note that the father is in the right place at the right time in this story. We learn in Proverbs 7:8–9 that it is nighttime. The father is not out wandering around because there is no reason to be out of his house late at night. The father is heeding his own instruction, and he is keeping far from the adulteress and not going near the door of her house (Proverbs 5:8–9). The father stays far away from temptation. He is not only giving his son good instruction, but he is also practicing the very wisdom that he is passing on to his son.

Fathers must heed this instruction and example today. It is good to stay far away from sexual temptation. It is good to be aware of how the devil will tempt you in different ways to succumb to sexual lust. It is not wise for a father to allow his teenage son to be alone in a room with a girl or to give his son access to the internet on phones, tablets, and TVs without carefully monitoring what the son may be exposed to. The father is to be an example for his son on keeping far away from temptation; he is to manage his household well and in such a way that keeps sexual temptation far from his son.

Third, the father introduces the foolish young man. The word the father uses to describe the young man comes from the original word *pthiy*, which can mean simple or foolish. This word can be used to describe someone who is impressionable and uninformed in judgment. In this context, it's used to describe someone who is morally deficient and spiritually vulnerable. In Proverbs, it's often used to describe someone who needs to heed God-given instruction.

This could be a young man who does not understand how the adulteress and sexual sin seduce, entice, and deceive. This could be a young man who does not understand the consequences of adultery and sexual sin or a young man who has not been instructed on how to avoid, flee, and abstain from sexual sin. In other words, this is a foolish young man who is vulnerable to the deception of sexual sin. However, this could also be a foolish young man who has been given godly instruction but is not yielding to this instruction. Whether he's not been instructed or he's not yielding to the instruction, he is a foolish young man.

Fourth, the father adds another element to his description of the foolish young man; he says that the young man is "*lacking understanding.*" The word for understanding comes from the original word *leb*; it is often used to describe the heart or mind, which is the center of a person's thoughts, emotions, will, and conscience. The father isn't saying that the young man doesn't have a heart or a mind. Rather, the father is saying that the young man has a heart or mind that has not been informed, trained, or shaped by the wisdom of God. This is Hebrew parallelism, which repeats an idea but states it in a different way. The young man is foolish because he lacks understanding. The young man lacks understanding because he is not trained in godly wisdom, and because he lacks godly wisdom, he is foolish and simple. This hearkens back to the instruction the father gives the son in Proverbs 7:1–5 where he tells the son to keep his words, treasure up his commandments, live, keep his teaching as precious, bind them on his fingers, write them on the tablet of his heart, and make wisdom his friend. It is just as deadly for the son to not be instructed in godly wisdom as it is for the son to be instructed but not keep, internalize, cherish, and obey the father's commands and fall into sexual sin.

> *Passing along the street near her corner, taking the road to her house in the twilight, in the evening, at the time of night and darkness.*
>
> —Proverbs 7:8–9

Fifth, we see the calamity of the foolish young man who strays into the path of the adulteress. In Proverbs 5:8–9, we learned that the son was to stay far away from the adulteress and not go near the door of her house. In our survey of the New Testament, we also learned that the son is to abstain from sexual immorality (1 Thessalonians 4:3) and keep from it so that he is not tempted and does not begin to lust in his heart (Proverbs 5:25, Matthew 5:28). Additionally, we learned that if he is being tempted or is coming close to sexual sin and temptation, he is to flee for his life (1 Corinthians 6:18). Proverbs 7:8–9 tells us that instead of staying far away, abstaining from, and fleeing from the adulteress and sexual sin, the young man is passing along the street and going near sexual temptation.

Sixth, we see that the foolish young man is at the wrong place at the wrong time. We've already established that the young man should have remained far away from the adulteress and sexual sin. However, now we learn that he is not where he should be. The workday in ancient Israel would have been from sunrise to sunset. The young man is not in the streets performing work, labor, or other tasks that are performed during the typical workday. Rather, he is out where he should not be and at the wrong time of day. This time at night would typically be used for rest, sleep, study, daily household obligations, and communal bonding. However, we see the young man being where he should not be and unaware and ignorant of the danger he has put himself into.

Seventh, notice the devastation of fathers not instructing their sons on the dangers of sexual sin and adultery. The foolish young man's father is not in this story, so we can't draw definite conclusions on what the foolish young man has been taught by his father. However, what we can deduce is that the foolish young man was either not instructed by his father or did not listen to, keep, obey, or cherish the instruction that he may have received. If the young foolish man did not receive instruction from his father, we should be deeply concerned because this young man is walking right into danger, and the father has not instructed, warned, or exhorted his son of these dangers. Is it the son who is responsible for this disaster, or is it the father? The answer is both.

As we've seen in Proverbs, it is the responsibility of the father and mother to instruct their sons regarding this danger. It is the father's responsibility to bring up their children in the discipline and instruction of the Lord (Ephesians 6:4). Yes, the son will be responsible for his sin, but it is also true that the father is held responsible for not instructing his son. There is no excuse for the father saying, "It was too embarrassing to talk about this subject," or "It was too uncomfortable to speak about sexual sin," or "Instructing my son on this danger wasn't that important." Such answers betray a lazy and apathetic heart. If you are a father or mother who refuses to instruct your children in the instruction of the Lord, repent!

> *And behold, the woman meets him, dressed as a prostitute, wily of heart.*
>
> —Proverbs 7:10

Eighth, the father calls the son to stop and pause, saying, "And behold." This instruction is not for nothing; it has purpose. It's as if the father is saying, "And now stop, behold, and see for yourself the result of lacking godly wisdom!" Because the foolish young man lacked knowledge, we will now see all the father's instruction come to a climax. The godly wisdom and instruction the father gave to his son concerning the adulteress's deceitful machinations, the consequences of sexual sin, and the tragedy of lacking wisdom will all be demonstrated in this encounter.

Ninth, notice that the adulteress comes to meet the foolish young man dressed as a prostitute to cause lust in his heart. Why is she described as being dressed as a prostitute rather than just in normal attire? Why is she dressed this way when she's married? As we learned earlier from the father's instruction, she uses her beauty, physical appearance, and seductive mannerisms to produce lust in the heart (Proverbs 6:25). Her wardrobe is not an accident. Her seductive mannerisms aren't a mishap. Not at all. She is dressed as a prostitute to appeal to the lust of the flesh (1 John 2:16). She does not adorn herself modestly (1 Timothy 2:9). Her attire is not meant to stir up wholesome and godly thoughts, but rather to feed the desires of the flesh such as sexual immorality, impurity, and sensuality (Galatians 5:19). Little does the foolish young man know that the adulteress has purposefully dressed seductively to stir up the passions of his flesh and is waging war against his soul (1 Peter 2:11).

Tenth, we see the adulteress has a deceptive heart. The word for deceptive comes from the original word *natsar*, which conveys something being guarded or kept and can be used positively or negatively. In this context it is used negatively. Her heart is guarded, secretive, and wily. She is not out to protect the foolish young man; she is set on deceiving him. As we learned in Proverbs 6:24, she is evil. She is not neutral or misguided. Rather, she is evil and wicked. She rejoices in the very things that God hates, and she does it all under a cloud of deception. Thus, she comes to the foolish young man, dressed as a prostitute, with a deceptive heart bent on capturing him.

> *She is loud and wayward; her feet do not stay at home.*
>
> —Proverbs 7:11

Eleventh, the adulteress is described as loud, which implies that she is boisterous and shameless. She does not possess godly characteristics such as having respectful and pure conduct (1 Peter 3:2). She does not have the inner beauty of a gentle and quiet spirit, which is precious in God's sight (1 Peter 3:4). She does not submit to her husband as godly and holy women are called to do (1 Peter 3:5–6); she is pictured as loud and self-willed. Rather than being loyal, she is loud, untamed, and unsubmissive. As we'll see, her outward actions reflect what is in her deceitful heart.

Twelfth, we see that she is rebellious. The ESV translates the word *carar* as wayward; the original word for *carar* also means rebellious, or stubborn. This word conveys willful resistance; it does not depict someone who disobeys out of ignorance. Rather, this word depicts someone who consciously, willfully, and purposefully rebels. The adulteress rebels against her husband by committing adultery; she rebels against God by breaking his commands. Thus, the adulteress is not characterized as some misinformed misfit. No, she is willfully and purposefully rebelling against her husband and against God.

Thirteenth, we see that she strays from her home and her God-given responsibilities as a wife. She is not a woman her husband can trust (Proverbs 31:11); she does her husband harm rather than good (Proverbs 31:12). She does not rise at night to provide food for her household; instead, she rises at night to indulge in sexual immorality (Proverbs 31:15). She is not working with her hands at night to provide and establish her household; she rises at night to wander the streets looking for foolish men (Proverbs 31:15). She does not open her mouth and speak wisdom; she opens her mouth and speaks deception (Proverbs 31:26). She does not fear the Lord but uses deceptive charm and vain beauty to entice (Proverbs 31:30). She is loud rather than gentle. The adulteress does the very opposite actions of the wife of noble character (Proverbs 31:10–31). She is characterized as straying from her home rather than fearing the Lord and supporting her husband and children.

> *Now in the street, now in the market, and at every corner she lies in wait.*
>
> —Proverbs 7:12

Fourteenth, we see that the adulterous woman is always available. The father says that she is in the street, in the market, and at every corner. This is just another way of saying that she's always available to seduce, tempt, and lead men into sexual sin. Whether she's going about her day in the street, in the open plaza for trade or worship, or wherever she is stalking, she is ready to use her cunning and deceptive seductions to entice. Just as the adulteress is available at all times and at all places, we should not be surprised that we find lewd and sexually charged images, videos, and social media everywhere. It should be no surprise that we see both men and women dressing provocatively in public or that clothing, which was once deemed inappropriate is now the norm. This is not by accident. Satan, who is called the devil (Matthew 4:1), the evil one (Matthew 13:19), the tempter (Matthew 4:3), the ruler of this world (John 14:30), the god of this age (2 Corinthians 4:4), the prince of the power of the air (Ephesians 2:2), the accuser of the brethren (Revelations 12:10), the old serpent (Revelation 12:9), the great dragon (Revelation 12:9), the roaring lion (1 Peter 5:8), Apollyon (Revelation 9:11), the father of lies (John

8:44), the antichrist (1 John 4:3), the ruler of the demons (Matthew 9:34), an angel of light (2 Corinthians 11:14), and more is the one who controls the wicked world system. Satan is opposed to everything that is good, and he seeks to turn that which is good to evil. Satan loves pornography, homosexual marriage, the LGBTQ movement, gender fluidity, fornication, and every sexually deviant and sinful thought, act, or intent. Just as the adulterous woman is available at all times and in all places, we should not be surprised that we see pornography so easily available and sexually charged media inundating us everywhere because it is Satan who seeks to tempt, entice, and destroy mankind in all places. The adulterer and the adulteress are available in the workplace, in the neighborhood, in the church, and everywhere else.

Fifteenth, notice that the father characterizes the adulteress as a predator; her actions are described as lurking. The word *lurking* comes from the original word *arab,* which can mean ambush, or lie in wait. This word conveys the idea of lying in wait or setting an ambush with hostile intent. Additionally, the word *lurking* is written in the imperfect aspect, which simply means that this is an incomplete action and implies that she never stops lurking. As we learned earlier, the father warned the son regarding how the adulterous woman seduces, entices, and tempts. She is pictured as a predator who stalks the streets, looks for prey, and is ready to attack at a moment's notice. Once again, we should not be surprised by her schemes. She is an unbeliever and under the prince of the power of the air (Ephesians 2:2). Just as the devil is a roaring lion seeking someone to devour, so is the adulterous woman (1 Peter 5:8). She is continually on the prowl and on the hunt looking for someone to devour.

> *She seizes him and kisses him, and with bold face she says to him, "I had to offer sacrifices, and today I have paid my vows; so now I have come out to meet you, to seek you eagerly, and I have found you.*
>
> —Proverbs 7:13–15

Sixteenth, we see that the predator seizes the prey. As we noted earlier, the picture that the father paints is one of a predator and prey. The adulteress has hidden motives and uses seduction and enticement; she's pictured as lurking, and now she's described as catching or seizing the foolish young man. This imagery is meant to be a horrifying picture. A lion prowls around at night, looks for wounded prey, targets individual prey, and seeks out the weak or vulnerable. When the lion attacks, it makes a killing bite to the back of the neck, spine, or throat. The father uses similar imagery. When he says that the adulteress seizes the foolish young man and kisses him, we are to have the same frightened response that we would have if a lion were to attack and seize a zebra. It is the horror of watching an alligator grab a gazelle and drag it to its death. The father is not telling the son a fairytale. The father is telling the son a horror story. This is the horror of being in the wrong place, at the wrong time, with no godly wisdom, and being attacked by a foe with overwhelming power. This is the dread we are supposed to see and feel.

Seventeenth, the adulteress uses physical touch to seduce the foolish young man. We saw that the adulteress uses physical touch and appeals to the physical senses in Proverbs 5:3 where it says, "*For the* ***lips of a forbidden woman drip honey****, and her speech is smoother than oil*" (emphasis added). In chapter 2, we discussed how this could be in reference to deceptive speech or to physical touch. Here, in Proverbs 7:13–15, we see the adulteress uses kisses and physical touch to entice the young man. Let's pause to consider how the adulteress has attacked the physical senses of the foolish young man. In Proverbs 7:10, she appealed to his eyes and vision by dressing like a prostitute. We now see that she uses physical touch to appeal to the foolish young man. The young man is having his physical senses and his flesh attacked and overloaded with sight and touch, which are meant to overcome him with lust. For men and women, it is important to know that physical touch and sight can be powerful tools to create sexual lust and temptation and overtake someone. This foolish young man serves as an example of someone whose physical senses are being attacked and overcome, but he is unaware of how he's being overcome and attacked.

Eighteenth, the adulterous woman deceives under the pretense of being religious but has a seared conscience and does not know the Lord even though she says that she has offered sacrifices and paid her vows. In the original language, the word *shelem* is used to describe the offering as a peace offering. The peace offering, also known as the fellowship offering, is a voluntary sacrifice. It is detailed in Leviticus 3:1–17 and 7:11–21, which is offered as an expression of thankfulness (Leviticus 7:12). It can also be offered as the result of a vow or a freewill offering (Leviticus 7:16). We also learn that the fellowship offering included the sacrifice of an animal (Leviticus 3:1–6); therefore, we should see the absolute perverted hypocrisy of the adulterous woman.

The fellowship offering was meant to bring the worshipper to repentance as the symbolic gesture of placing one's hand on the head of the animal was to show the transfer of sins from the one sacrificing the animal to the sacrificial animal (Leviticus 3:2). The sacrifice of the animal was not to invoke spiritual pride and righteousness; it was a symbolic gesture meant to bring about repentance. The transferring of sin to the sacrificial animal was to bring about sorrow for sin against the Lord and teach His people that the penalty for sin is death. The sacrificial system was meant to show the Israelites the consequences of sin, the holiness of God, and the need for a substitutionary propitiation for their sins. However, the adulterous woman can go through a ritual that is meant to bring her to repentance, but she has such a seared conscience that she can't see her own sin or the holiness of God. Thus, she treats sin as trivial, demonstrating that she does not know God even though she goes through the sacrificial ritual.

Additionally, she says that she has paid her vows. The fellowship offering could be given as a vow. The greatest example of this is when Hannah prays and pours her soul out to the Lord for a son because she is barren (1 Samuel 1:1–20). Hannah made a vow that if the Lord gave her a son, she would give the son to the Lord for all the days of his life and he would never put a razor to his head (1 Samuel 1:11). After Hannah becomes pregnant, she gives birth to Samuel and offers a fellowship offering (1 Samuel 1:21–28). Hannah's plea for a son, her vow, and her sacrifice were God-pleasing. However, the adulteress perverts the fellowship offering. This is the absolute perverse and disgraceful religious hypocrisy of the adulterous woman. The adulterous woman proclaims that she has done her religious duty and been faithful to God; she has sought for the young man, and the Lord has answered her prayer. It's as if she's saying, "I have made a sacrifice to God, made a vow, and prayed to God that He would send me you, and behold, He has answered my prayer!" This is utterly disgraceful. She's essentially saying, "I've offered my fellowship offering, prayed for a young man to commit adultery with, and the Lord sent me you." The adulteress uses deception to make it seem like this encounter is the will of God and an answer to prayer. As the father warned the son earlier, the adulteress does not ponder the path of life; her ways wander, and she does not know the path of life (Proverbs 5:6). Her deceptive religious talk is evidence of her evil and deceitful character.

Recall that in 1 Thessalonians 4:3, it is the will of God that believers be sanctified and abstain from sexual immorality.

Many churchgoing people speak religious talk, are members of churches, and are active in the church, but they live lives of sexual immorality. They may go to church, but behind closed doors they are unrepentantly indulging in pornography, fornication, and other immoral acts. Let us learn from the adulteress that Satan is perfectly pleased with churchgoing and religious-sounding hypocrites who lead secret lives of sexual immorality.

> *I have spread my couch with coverings, colored linens from Egyptian linen.*
>
> —Proverbs 7:16

Nineteenth, the adulteress appeals to the foolish young man's mind. What does the adulterous woman immediately turn the foolish young man's mind to? What is it she wants him to think about? It is her bed. Not only does she begin filling his thoughts of her and her bed, but she also begins describing her bed. She says that she has put colored Egyptian linen coverings on her bed. This is all meant to appeal to the lust of the flesh. The young man has now seen the adulteress dressed as a prostitute, been kissed by her, touched by her, told that he is an answer to her prayers, and now she fills his mind with thoughts of her bed, which is adorned with comfortable and beautiful linen. Egyptian linen was considered comfortable because it was lightweight and breathable in an arid and hot climate. She has filled his mind with thoughts of her body, thoughts of physical intimacy, and thoughts of comfortable bedding. We can clearly see that the adulteress is drowning the foolish young man in lustful thoughts.

The twentieth point we should see is that the adulteress is comfortable with making lewd comments with the greatest of ease. Instead of being modest in her speech, she is crass and is adept at taking conversations to base and crude levels. We see this in that she purposefully discusses the arrangements of her bed or "couch." This is completely vulgar. We should not talk about the bed or bedroom with a stranger. Proverbs 4:24 says that you should "*put away from you* ***crooked speech,*** *and put devious talk far from you.*" Additionally, in Ephesians 4:29, it says, "*Let no* ***corrupting talk*** *come out of your mouths, but only such as is good for building up, as fits the occasion, that it may give grace to those who hear*" (emphasis added). The word for corrupting talk comes from the original word *sapros,* which means that which is rotten, bad, or corrupt; it conveys the idea of something that has suffered decay and is putrid and rendered toxic. Talking about one's bedroom with a stranger is not straight talk, it is crooked speech. It is speech that corrupts the mind rather than building up one's thoughts in godliness.

Additionally, Ephesians 5:4 says that Christians are to "*let there be no* ***filthiness*** *nor* ***foolish talk*** *nor* ***crude joking,*** *which are out of place, but instead let there be thanksgiving*" (emphasis added). The word for *filthiness* comes from the original word *aischrotés,* which speaks of language that is shameful, obscene, and base; such language is shameful, vulgar, and despised even in social settings. The word for foolish talk comes from the original word *mórologia* and refers to the speech of morons and that which is empty and senseless. Lastly, the word for crude joking comes from the original word *eutrapelia,* which speaks of coarse joking, which is improper and immodest.

Crooked speech, corrupting talk, filthy language, foolish talk, and crude joking that are sexual in nature are all telltale signs of someone in the throes of sexual sin. It is a person who is comfortable with bringing conversations to a base level. They tend to make inappropriate sexual jokes and ask questions about private details that have no business being discussed. They show no shame in making crude comments, and they have a fascination and disposition to talk about sexually charged topics. They push the limits of what is considered appropriate conversation. Beware of such a person, for they speak from the overflow of their heart (Luke 6:45). People who eagerly take conversations to sexually deviant levels must be avoided.

> *I have perfumed my bed with myrrh, aloes, and cinnamon.*
>
> —Proverbs 7:17

The twenty-first point we should see is that the adulteress appeals to the young man's sense of smell. Let's review again how she has attacked the foolish young man's senses. First, she attacked his thoughts; next, she attacked his vision with her provocative wardrobe, and now she attacks his sense of smell and with enticing aromas. Once again, she brings the foolish young man back to thoughts of the bed, and now she says that her bed not only feels and looks good, but it also smells good. Everything is meant to attack every thought and sense of the young man. It is meant to overwhelm him to the point that he can't say no and gives into sin. The adulteress is very skilled at appealing to the lust of the flesh, which includes his mental and physical senses.

> *Come, let us take our fill of love till morning; let us delight ourselves with love.*
>
> —Proverbs 7:18

The twenty-second point we should note is that she calls lust, love. As we learned earlier, the father wants his son to know that physical intimacy is to be enjoyed and fulfilled only within the confines of marriage between a man and a woman (Proverbs 5:18–19). The father wants the son to know he can enjoy and be intoxicated with the physical intimacy of his wife, and that this is a form of biblical love between a husband and a wife. The father even warns the son that no good can come from being intoxicated with an adulteress's body (Proverbs 5:20). However, we see the adulteress twist the meaning of love into lust. This is not love; it's adultery. This is not love; it's immorality. The adulteress deceives the foolish young man into thinking that relationship with her is actually love. She encourages him to delight and become filled, satiated, and satisfied with this form of physical intimacy, which is really immorality, adultery—that which God hates.

There are plenty of ways that today's society can turn love into lust; we see this in the form of many lies. A boyfriend and girlfriend will justify living together, lie, and justify that this arrangement is OK because they need to save and be responsible with money. Engaged couples live together prior to marriage and justify this immoral arrangement because they love each other and intend to be married. Unmarried churchgoing couples unrepentantly fornicate with one another and ignorantly claim, "Justification by faith alone and not by works!" and "He who is without sin cast the first stone!" These excuses and lies are the very tools the devil and the adulteress use to tempt mankind into sexual sin, skillfully turning the meaning of love into lust.

> *For my husband is not at home; he has gone on a long journey; he took a bag of money with him; at full moon he will come home.*
>
> —Proverbs 7:19–20

The twenty-third point we should see is that the adulteress is unfaithful to her husband because she has a low view of marriage and low view of her husband. She is not a wife who respects and honors her husband. She is a wife who cannot be trusted, is unfaithful to her marital covenant, and despises her husband.

The twenty-fourth point we see is that she deceives the foolish young man into thinking that God would not see this act of immorality, which gives evidence that she does not know God. One of the attributes of God is that He is omnipresent, which means that He is present everywhere at the same time because He is not limited by time or space. Several verses, including Proverbs 15:3, speak of God's omnipresence: "*The eyes of the Lord are in every place, keeping watch on the evil and the good.*" The adulterous woman's foolishness show that she does not know God. Perhaps she believes that the cover of night hides her sin but does not realize that it is exposed and laid bare before Him to whom she must give an account (Hebrews 4:13). She makes no mention that God would see the seductive act she has planned. Though she speaks of God, she does not know Him; she doesn't understand that the act of adultery will one day be judged. She pays no attention to God and does not know of His holiness and glory. Rather, she is only concerned with fulfilling her lustful intentions and hiding this sin from her husband. There are many men in the church that have this mindset. They look at pornography and fornicate outside of marriage without realizing that they will one day give an account to the omnipresent and omniscient triune God.

The twenty-fifth point to note is that she has a low view of her personal sin. Not only does the adulteress not know the holiness, wrath, righteousness, and omniscience of God, but she also has a low view and warped understanding of sin. She can brazenly invite the foolish young man into her house to commit adultery the very same day that she had offered a fellowship offering. Thus, she doesn't truly see her sin as an offense to God. She doesn't understand that this act of immorality deserves death or that God will judge the adulterer and the sexually immoral person (Hebrews 13:4). She sees her sin as light and trivial rather than something that God abhors (Psalm 5:4–5). Be aware of such a person who trivializes sin, downplays immorality, and makes excuses for their sinful sexual behavior. Beware of pastors who downplay the dangers of sexual sin and those who are ensnared to it as they proclaim, "You are justified by faith and not by works." People who have such a low view of sin give evidence that they may not know God, or they may simply be immature Christians who are in need of much growth. Beware of your own personal thoughts when you start making excuses for looking at sexually charged videos and pictures. Beware when you make excuses and downplay fantasizing and lusting in the heart. Do not call sin your "friend" and become desensitized to it. Beware when you begin calling sin something less than what it is, which is falling short of God's glory and a form of rebellion against Him.

The twenty-sixth point we notice is that the adulteress is very calculating in her act of sexual sin. She states that her husband has gone on a long journey, and she knows precisely when he will return. Thus, she is very deliberate and intentional to commit adultery when the right time arises. She is pernicious and evil in her calculated and methodical timing. As we learned earlier, she operates in secrecy and under the cloak of night. Beware of those who are out late at night and have secret and hidden lifestyles. This does not mean that everyone who is out late or has a secret lifestyle is sexually immoral. However, let's note that the sexually immoral are calculating about when, where, and how they commit their sin. Beware of those who are secretive with their phones, tablets, and personal electronic devices. Those who indulge in sexual immorality are calculated in when, where, and how they gratify their lusts.

> *With much seductive speech she persuades him; with her smooth talk she compels him.*
>
> —Proverbs 7:21

The twenty-seventh point of note is that her smooth and flattering speech has tempted, seduced, enticed, manipulated, and persuaded the foolish young man to give in to the adulteress. She has plied every weapon within her arsenal and persuaded the foolish young man with her lies. It's important to note that the stem of the verb *compels him* is a causative stem, which means that the adulteress has caused the seduction to happen. She has skillfully and deceptively caused the young man to fall into her trap. In the graphic below, we see how she deceived the young foolish man with touch, sight, lies, thoughts, and smell.

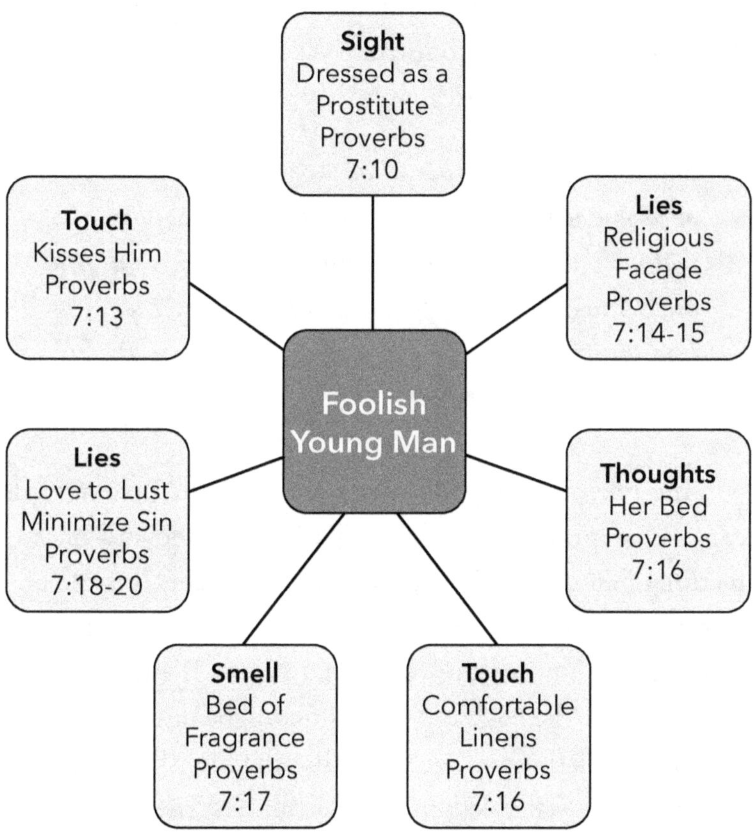

The twenty-eighth point is that the young man is truly foolish and simple. Either he has not been instructed in godly wisdom regarding sexual sin, or he has blatantly chosen to ignore or reject godly wisdom. The young man was tempted, lured, and enticed by his own desire, which led to sin (James 1:14–15). The young man didn't abstain from, flee from, or stay far away from sexual sin and temptation; he did not follow any of the godly wisdom we've seen given thus far. Therefore, it comes as no surprise that he has been persuaded to fall into sexual sin because he is simple and foolish.

> *Suddenly he follows her as an ox goes to the slaughter, or as one walks in ankle bracelets to the discipline of a fool until an arrow pierces through his liver; as a bird hurries to the snare, so he does not know that it will cost him his life.*
>
> —Proverbs 7:22–23 NASB

The twenty-ninth point we see is that the predator has caught her prey. Once again, this is a horrific and ghastly picture of an ox being led to have its throat slit. It is the picture of someone receiving a death shot through the liver. It is imagery of a noose closing around a bird. The trap was set, the prey took the bait, and the result will be death.

The thirtieth point we see is that the foolish young man was completely helpless in this encounter. The father gives three analogies with two of the analogies picturing animals being caught. It is no accident that the father compares the foolish young man to a bird and an ox. Both the ox and the bird are non-predatory animals. In fact, the ox and the bird were both used in the Levitical sacrificial system because they were non-predatory animals. Just like the ox and the bird, the foolish young man is pictured as a defenseless animal that walks straight into a trap and into slaughter. The final analogy is a picture of a fool who is held in bondage and receives a kill shot to a vital organ, his liver. Thus, we see that the foolish young man is defenseless like a non-predatory animal and is easily executed like an ox to the slaughter or as someone being easily shot because he is physically held in bondage. Without godly wisdom and instruction, the foolish young man is defenseless against the wiles of the adulteress and sexual sin.

The thirty-first point is that the foolish young man does not know that this will cost him his life. As we learned earlier, the Old Testament penalty for adultery was stoning (Deuteronomy 22:22). We also learned that the young man would receive dishonor and shame (Proverbs 6:33), the wrath of the husband (Proverbs 6:31–35), the loss of labors and monetary wealth (Proverbs 6:10), the potential for venereal disease (Proverbs 5:11), the potential for being ensnared and enslaved to sexual sin (Proverbs 5:22), and destruction of his soul (Proverbs 6:32). What the young man thought would bring satisfaction will bring death, enslavement to sin, and other consequences.

Not only this, but Proverbs 22:14 makes this ominous statement: "*The mouth of an adulteress is a deep pit;* ***He who is cursed of the Lord will fall into it***" (NASB emphasis added). In other words, falling into continuous sexual sin strongly indicates that someone is an unbeliever, unregenerate, and cursed by the Lord. The word for *cursed* comes from the original word *za`am*, which can also mean abhorred, abominable, or angry with. Additionally, the word *fall* is written in the imperfect, which simply means that this is an incomplete action and implies that the person under the Lord's wrath continues to fall into sexual sin and the adulteress's trap. Not only this, but the person who falls into sexual sin is pictured as falling into a deep pit. This deep pit is not a little three foot hole. No, this is a picture of falling into a deep pit where escape may not be possible. This pictures the extreme difficulty of escaping once entrapped. It is possible that true believers can become ensnared, and by God's grace, escape. However, let's give Proverbs 22:14 its proper weight. The one who continues to fall into sexual sin indicates he is cursed and abhorred by the Lord and may never escape; they may come to eternal ruin. This is why the father instructs his son to abstain and flee from sexual sin. It is a deadly sin that entangles and may cost someone their life and their soul.

The last point that should be made is that sexual sin leads to darker and grosser sin. What does this mean? It is not unusual to hear of men who saw a pornographic image become curious and begin to seek more pornographic images. The habit of looking at pornographic images turns into watching pornographic videos. This leads to deviant images and videos that desensitize the conscience to sin. This, in turn, can lead to acting out these sins in the form of self-gratification, fornication, adultery, and other deviant and sinful acts. If a man becomes enslaved to these sins while he is unmarried, he will inevitably bring these sins into his marriage because he is entangled and ensnared and has learned to hide them. Eventually, these sins lead to physical adultery and the devastation of his marriage. As we mentioned earlier, sin will take you further than you ever wanted to go, keep you longer than you ever wanted to stay, and cost you more than you ever thought you would pay. The father in Proverbs knows that sexual sin can cost someone their life. No biblical father would ever want to see their sons or daughters be ensnared by this type of sin.

In this chapter, we have walked through the powerful story the father gives to the son regarding the dangers and consequences of the adulteress and sexual sin. We saw the adulteress's evil schemes, deceptions, and machinations, which captured the foolish young man. The father uses this story as a powerful teaching tool for the son; it has the perfect balance of a detailed and instructive story that preserves the son's conscience and is absent of graphic and perverse detail. It is a magnificent story in that it takes sexual sin seriously and stresses the importance of cherishing godly wisdom for the sake of one's life and soul. It is a glorious story that a loving Christian father can tell his son to keep his son far away from the adulteress and sexual sin. Would a loving Christian father withhold this instruction from his son? King Solomon and the Triune God have emphatically declared that loving fathers include this godly wisdom and instruction to their sons.

Chapter 4

The Father's Final Commands and Warnings to the Son

In chapter 4, we will review the father's final commands and closing statements to his son. In Proverbs 7:24–25, the father gives the son four commands and three indicative statements regarding those that the adulteress has slain and the destiny of those who give into her temptation. This is a serious and somber ending to the father's instruction. Anyone who is reading carefully can clearly see that the father's instruction is a matter of life and death. Let us keep the father's instruction, warnings, admonitions, and story that we've seen in Proverbs chapter 2, 5, 6, and 7 at the front of our mind as we examine the last four verses of Proverbs chapter 7:

> *And now, O sons, listen to me, and be attentive to the words of my mouth. Let not your heart turn aside to her ways; do not stray into her paths.*
>
> —Proverbs 7:24–25

In these verses, we see that the father draws a conclusion to all his instructions. The father's first two commands are positive exhortations to listen to his instruction; he wants the son to consider all his teaching, instruction, warning, and exhortations and give them all the weighty meditation they deserve. The father's first two commands include the words, "***listen*** *to me*" and "***be attentive*** *to the words of my mouth*" (emphasis added). Both verbs are written in the imperative, which means these are commands. The first word *listen* conveys the idea of listening in such a way that the person intellectually comprehends and submits morally and volitionally. The father is not commanding the son to listen to his words just to hear himself talk; he is commanding the son to listen for the sake of his life. The phrase *be attentive* conveys the idea of concentrated listening to yield the appropriate response. Once again, this is Hebrew parallelism, which states the same idea, but in a nuanced way.

The last two commands that the father gives the son are negative exhortations on what the son is to avoid: The son is not to let his heart turn aside to the adulteress's ways or to stray into her paths. The father's command is that the son would not lust in his heart and that he would abstain and flee from the adulteress and sexual immorality. Thus, the father's last four commands include two positive exhortations to follow godly wisdom and two negative commands to avoid sexual sin and temptation.

These last four commands capture all the father's instruction regarding sexual sin and marriage presented thus far in

Proverbs 2, 5, 6, and 7. If we reflect on everything that's been said, we could paraphrase the father's final instruction as follows:

> My son, keep my words, treasure up my commands, cherish my commandments and live (Proverbs 7:1–3). Apply my instruction to your life; internalize and meditate upon my commands, and do not forsake my teaching. Make wisdom precious and call it your friend (Proverbs 7:4–5). I have given you all these instructions to keep you far away from sexual sin. I have told you how the adulteress will deceive with smooth words (Proverbs 2:16), seduce with her lips (Proverbs 5:3), lie with her speech (Proverbs 5:4), dress provocatively (Proverbs 7:10), abandon and betray her husband (Proverbs 7:18–20), speak religious talk but will not know God (Proverbs 7:14–15), entice your senses and fleshly desires with lustful pleasures and thoughts (Proverbs 7:16–17), twist love into lust (Proverbs 7:18), and cause you to lust for her beauty in your heart (Proverbs 6:25).
>
> My son, remember what you have learned about the consequences of indulging in sexual sin. Remember that the consequences of committing sexual sin could be physical, emotional, or spiritual (Proverbs 6:27–28); you may have to give your wealth and labor to others (Proverbs 5:10), and you may

suffer from physical disease that ravages your body and causes you sorrow and regret (Proverbs 5:11). Remember that you will receive shame, dishonor, and blows (Proverbs 6:33), and you may have to face the wrathful vengeance of the adulteress's husband (Proverbs 6:34–35). Remember that the Lord sees everything (Proverbs 5:21). Remember that sexual sin can capture, ensnare, and hold you in bondage (Proverbs 5:22); those who commit sexual sin and adultery destroy themselves and their souls (Proverbs 6:32, 1 Peter 2:11).

My dear son, remember that physical intimacy should be enjoyed only between husband and wife in the confines of marriage (Proverbs 5:18–19). You are to love your wife as Christ loved the church and gave Himself for her (Ephesians 5:25).

My dear son, do not forget the story of the foolish young man who was caught by the adulteress; don't forget how she caught him. My son, cherish godly wisdom. When you see the adulteress, sexual sin, or are tempted with lust, abstain and flee from all forms of sexual immorality and deal radically and repentantly with sin (Proverbs 7:25, 6:25, 1 Thessalonians 4:3, 1 Corinthians 6:18, Matthew 5:28–30). Trust in the Lord with all your heart and lean not on your own understanding; in all your ways acknowledge him, and he will make your paths straight and do not be wise in your own eyes; fear the Lord and shun evil (Proverbs 3:5–7).

For many are the victims she has brought to ruin, and numerous are all those slaughtered by her. Her house is the way to Sheol, descending to the chambers of death.

—Proverbs 7:26–27 NASB

In the final two verses, the father pictures the adulteress and sexual sin as a mighty enemy and powerful predator. The father acknowledges that the enemy is powerful by stating that she has many victims. The word for *many* comes from the original word *rab*, which conveys the idea of a multitude and abundance. Sexual sin is not an enemy that only captures a few. Not at all, it is pictured as a ruthless and devastating enemy. When people think of cancer, HIV, and heart disease, they think of life-threatening diseases that often overcome their victims. In the very same way, the adulteress and sexual sin are pictured as enemies who have brought many to devastation. The adulteress and sexual sin have led to many divorces, many broken homes, enslavement to pornography, sex trafficking, sexual abuse, incurable or deadly venereal diseases, rampant fornication and co-habitation of unmarried couples, and more. However, the most serious way the adulteress and sexual sin have brought many to ruin is by enslaving men to this sin where many perish in their sin and go to hell.

We also see that sexual sin and the adulteress don't just

cause weak and sinful men to fall, but sexual sin causes even mighty men to fall. In the original language, the word *numerous* is *`atsuwm,* which can also mean mighty or strong. David killed Goliath (1 Samuel 17), and it was said of David that he had slain tens of thousands (1 Samuel 18:7). However, we see that David, who was a man after God's heart who loved the Lord (1 Samuel 13:14) fell into sexual sin and adultery (2 Samuel 11). Samson was a physically strong man and who killed 1,000 men with the jawbone of a donkey, but he was laid low by Delilah (Judges 16). The Bible gives unapologetic evidence that sexual sin has the power to cause physically and spiritually strong men to fall. Even today we see many politically prominent men and women have their adulterous relationships made public; pastors are deposed for adulterous relationships or having pornography on their personal devices. A high percentage of professing Christian men claim to be addicted to pornography. The adulteress and sexual sin are a murderous predator. The father warns the son that even strong and mighty men have been slain and laid low by her deceitful and evil schemes.

Finally, the father describes the spiritual reality of going into the house of the adulteress or the house of sexual sin. While the adulteress describes her house as having comfortable linen, aromatic spices, the company of a seductively beautiful woman, the father paints a different reality. The spiritual reality is that when one goes into her house, he is walking into Sheol and descending into a house of death. The father pulls the veil away from the adulteress's lies so that instead of seeing the linens, spices, or a beautiful woman, the son sees death and a chamber of corpses. The adulteress's house contains the rotting corpses of a multitude of men who have been slain by sexual sin. This is vivid imagery to warn the son that sexual sin is deadly, not life-giving. For all who go into her domain, the way of the adulteress leads not to life but into the realm of the dead that is full of corpses of men that she has conquered and slain. What a picture the father gives to warn his son of the dangers of sexual sin!

Chapter 5

The Gospel: The Adulterer's and Adulteress's Only Hope

In chapters 1 through 4, we learned that if one simply lusts for someone in their heart, it is sin, and that is enough for them to be sentenced to eternity in hell (Matthew 5:28). Therefore, we must understand how to think about sexual sin in light of the gospel. Is someone saved because they never commit adultery (Exodus 20:14)? Is someone saved because they never once viewed pornographic material? Is someone saved based on their ability to keep the law? Is someone saved based on their Christian morality regarding sexual purity? The answer is a resounding no. There is no one who can say they have a pure heart and are clean from sin (Proverbs 20:9). If anyone fails to keep the law in one point, they are guilty of breaking the whole law (James 2:10). Therefore, the godly father knows that teaching on sexual sin does not produce righteousness. He knows that any teaching on the law and sin points to the need for a Lord and Savior.

Some people have very good marriages but have never come to true repentance and saving faith in Christ. There are people who live very moral lives, but they do not believe the gospel. Therefore, the godly father does not teach his son about the adulteress and sexual sin in the hope that the son will keep the law perfectly. Rather, the father instructs the son on sexual sin to keep him from the deadly consequences of sin, to teach him the fear of the Lord, and to show his son the need for the gospel and the need to trust in the Lord with all his heart. Without a saving knowledge of the Lord Jesus Christ, there is no hope for the son. Therefore, it is imperative that the father also teach his son the true gospel. We will dedicate this chapter to explaining the gospel, which includes the bad news of sin, the bad news of hell, the authority and sufficiency of Scripture, the person and work of Christ, and man's responsibility to respond in repentance and faith to the Lord Jesus Christ. We will do this by performing a brief exposition of Romans 1:1–6 and Matthew 16:24–26.

The Bad News – Sin

If we are to understand God's good news, then we must understand God's bad news. The bad news is not that we have credit card debt, a house payment, loss of a job, no food to eat, political issues, wars, a failing education system, illness, injury, bad in-laws, a car that won't run, low self-esteem, no friends, no spouse, no children, social inequality, income inequality, or any such thing. The bad news is that man has sinned against God, and God must deal with man's sin.

Therefore, we need to first define and understand sin. *Hamartía*, from which we get the word *sin* in the New Testament, carries the meaning of missing the mark or loss and forfeiture because of not hitting the target. Therefore, sin is characterized as missing the mark of God's holy moral standard and character. First John 3:4 helps us further define sin where it says, "*Everyone who makes a practice of sinning also practices lawlessness;* ***sin is lawlessness***" (emphasis added). Here the Apostle John describes sin as lawlessness. The original word for *lawlessness* comes from *anomia*, which is translated as lawlessness or anti-law. Thus, we can say that sin is lawlessness or disobedience against God's holy moral standard and character. John further defines sin in these words: "*All* ***unrighteousness is sin***" (1 John 5:17 NASB2020, emphasis added). The word *unrighteousness* comes to us from *adikia*, meaning injustice or wrongdoing. Sin is rightly described as injustice and wrongdoing against God because the sinner misses the mark of God's perfect law. Thus, sin is anything that does not conform to God's standard of righteousness and justice. James gives us yet another definition of sin in James 4:17: "*So whoever knows the right thing to do and fails to do it, for him it is sin.*"

Here we can see that sin is not only what we do to break God's law, but it also includes failing to do what God's law requires. Thus, a good definition of sin would be as follows: Sin is breaking God's law by either not doing what God's law demands or doing what God's law prohibits by any thought (Matthew 5:28), word (Matthew 5:22), deed (Matthew 5:39), or intent (Matthew 6:1).

Next, we must understand how the God of the Bible deals with sinners who have broken His law and offended Him. Quite simply, we learn that the God of the Bible deals with sinners according to who He is. First, we would need to know something of the attributes of God—that He is eternal, loving, just, good, faithful, omniscient, immutable, omnipresent, holy, and more. The attributes of God dictate the necessity for God to punish sinners who violate and break His law.

Since God is eternal and man has offended the eternal God (1 Timothy 1:17), the question is, "What is a just punishment for a finite man who sins against an infinite God?" The obvious answer is that the punishment must be eternal because God, the offended party, is the eternal God. Therefore, the penalty for man sinning against God demands an eternal punishment because God is eternal.

Since God is a loving God (1 John 4:17), there are things that God hates. For example, since God is the only true God, He hates idolatry because it robs Him of His glory. Because God loves truth, He hates falsehood and lies. Therefore, since God must hate evil because He is love, He must punish sinners who sin against Him and do the very things He hates because He is an eternal and loving God.

God is a just God, and man has offended Him by sinning against Him; therefore, God must deal equitably and justly with those who have broken His law (Ezekiel 18:1–32). It is simply not in God's character to leave sin unpunished. God deals justly and equitably with sin. God is not a corrupt judge who will ignore sin; He is not a biased judge who will overlook sin. The God of the Bible is a God who deals justly with sinners who commit the very sins He hates. Even unholy man knows that it would be unjust to pardon a serial murderer with no punishment. Thus, God must deal justly with the sinner and see to it that every sin the sinner commits is eternally and justly punished because He is an eternal, loving, and just God.

God is good; therefore, He must punish sin (Psalm 25:8). To leave sin unpunished would not be good; it would be bad, evil, and wicked. Even the unregenerate man knows that a parent who throws a newborn baby in a dumpster commits a wicked and murderous act, which must be punished; it would be wicked for a judge to freely pardon a parent for such an atrocity. God cannot let sin go unpunished. In His goodness, God must punish sin because He is an eternal, loving, just, and good God.

God is also holy, meaning that He is set apart, and there is nothing or no one like Him (Isaiah 44:6). He is totally separate in terms of all His attributes, which include His self-existence, sovereignty, immutability, self-sufficiency, omnipotence, omniscience, omnipresence, wisdom, faithfulness, goodness, justice, mercy, graciousness, love, and glory. It is quite clear, that all mankind is fallen and doesn't meet God's level of holiness and perfection (Romans 3:23). Therefore, God must punish mankind according to their sin because He is an eternal, loving, just, good, and holy God.

It is also important to understand how the God of the Bible views sin and those who sin against Him. The Bible tells us that God hates sin (Psalm 5:5, 11:5), abhors sin (Psalm 5:6), is angered by sin (Psalm 7:11), and is ready to destroy and punish those who sin (Psalm 7:12–13). We understand that any sin someone commits violates and rebels against God's holy moral standard. God considers all sin as warfare against Him (James 4:4); He considers sin an abomination (Proverbs 22:12) and evil (Psalm 7:9). Because God hates sin, He must deal with sin according to who He is. For God to leave sin unpunished would violate and be in opposition to His character. Knowing that the God of the Bible must punish sin, we need to understand how God punishes sin. The God of the Bible does not change; He will always hate sin. The God who sent a flood to destroy humanity and left only eight survivors is the same God of the New Testament. The God who sent burning sulfur down on Sodom and Gomorrah and destroyed an entire city will never change in His anger against sin.

The Bible also teaches that God punishes sinners by sending them to hell. The doctrine of hell is quite possibly one of the least favorite and least taught doctrines in Scripture.

However, it is a doctrine that must be covered because it makes the glory of the gospel and Christ shine even brighter. The bad news of hell is more than bad news; it is terrifying. The bad news from God about hell is the worst news possible for sinful man.

The godly father is not to leave out this doctrine when instructing his son. The father is to teach the son about the punishment and horrors of hell and the necessity for God to send sinners to hell if they refuse to repent and put their faith in Christ. All parents need to teach their children about the doctrine of hell. All churches need to teach about the doctrine of hell. All pastors need to teach about the doctrine of hell.

The Bad News – Hell

Although this section cannot cover every aspect of the doctrine of hell, it will be thorough enough for the reader to understand the horrors of hell because as we've learned, the godly father does not withhold instruction on the consequences of sin.

John the Baptist describes hell as a place of fire where every tree that does not bear fruit of repentance is cut down and thrown into the fire (Matthew 3:11). Jesus describes hell as a furnace of fire, which pictures a concentrated fire (Matthew 13:42). The author of Hebrews describes hell as a place that contains furious fire that consumes and devours the enemies of God (Hebrews 10:27). Therefore, we know that hell is a place full of the omnipotent, wild, and zealous fire of God that consumes His enemies. The Bible does not give a picture of hell as a warm sauna or a nice warm campfire. Wildfires that ravage and consume everything in their way are nothing compared to the fires of hell. Volcanoes that gush forth red hot lava are nothing compared to the omnipotent, unmitigated, unquenchable, and unrestrained fires of hell. Thus, the Bible describes hell as a place that burns with a wild and zealous fire that eternally and perpetually consumes and devours sinners with the omnipotent heat and righteous anger of God.

John the Baptist describes hell as eternal in that the fire never goes out but burns forever (Matthew 3:12). Jesus describes hell as being so horrible that it must be avoided at all costs when He says that it would be better to lose one of your members than to be thrown into hell (Matthew 5:29–30). Jesus said that just one sin is enough to merit someone being cast into hell (Matthew 5:28) because even one offense against God requires His punishment. Jesus describes hell as a place of weeping and gnashing of teeth, which means it is a place where the sinner is in an eternal state of anger against God and unfathomable sadness and despair (Matthew 8:12). Jesus describes hell as a place of destruction where one's whole body and soul are being eternally destroyed by the omnipotent and unrestrained wrath of God (Matthew 7:13, 10:28); it is a place where the whole of a man—body, soul, and spirit—is eternally being destroyed by the unmitigated and all-powerful wrath of God.

After death, unrepentant man does not go into state of annihilation; nor does he go out of existence. He goes into an eternal state where his body, soul, and spirit are continually being destroyed; Jesus describes hell as inescapable (Luke 16:26). In hell, the sinner will realize that the time to respond to the gospel has passed. In hell, a person will have full awareness that after one trillion years of torment, that one trillion years will be like a drop in the ocean compared to eternity. After one trillion years in hell, there will only be an infinite number of trillion years for the unrepentant sinner to suffer in hell.

Jesus describes hell as being full of excruciating pain with no reprieve (Luke 16:24). Though man will desire the goodness that God gives in water, air, rest, and comfort, the man will find no such comfort for even a millisecond for all eternity. Hell is described by Jesus as a place that is full of mental anguish and torment—a place where there is only regret, sorrow, and haunting memories of rejecting Christ (Luke 16:25). All the debauched pleasures and self-deception that the man indulged in will give him no comfort. The lost opportunity and eternal regret of neglecting or rejecting Christ will be his haunting memory forever. Jude describes hell as the blackest darkness, which describes a place of such appalling gloom and a darkness that can be felt (Jude 13). A hopeless and despairing darkness is what awaits man in hell.

Hell is also described as a place where man will have personal punishments and that every sin ever committed by the sinner will be paid back in full retribution by God (Romans

2:5). In fact, Psalm 94:1–2 describes the Lord as the God of vengeance where it says, "*O Lord, **God of vengeance**, O **God of vengeance**, shine forth! Rise up, O judge of the earth; repay to the proud what they deserve*" (emphasis added)! To God, no sin is small. No sin is forgotten. No sin is erased by good works. No sin is overlooked. The God of the Bible takes immaculate and perfect record of all sins. Every sin that the unrepentant nonbeliever commits is storing up wrath, blows, punishment, torment, and vengeance that the Lord will repay. In fact, the God of the Bible is described as personally repaying and settling accounts with men face to face; Deuteronomy 7:10 says that "[He] ***repays to their face*** *those who hate him,* ***by destroying them****. He will not be slack with one who hates him.* ***He will repay him to his face***" (emphasis added). God is personal in his retribution; He is personal in his vengeance. Every blow and lash will be perfectly administered in hell (Luke 12:47). The omnipotent and unbridled temperature of the furnace of fire will be personally determined by God and will eternally consume His adversaries (Hebrews 10:27). God will see to it that the unrepentant unbeliever is cut to pieces, bound hand and foot, and thrown into hell (Matthew 22:13, 24:51). God will see to it that the unrepentant unbeliever is encased and swallowed up in perpetual darkness and gloom with no hope of escape (Matthew 22:13). This is the awful and fearful reality of the unrepentant unbeliever falling into the hands of the living God (Hebrews 10:31). Vengeance belongs to the Lord, and He will repay with devastating and unfathomable divine retribution that man cannot comprehend. The hands of the living God that are a source of security and refuge for the believer (John 10:28–29) are the same hands that will deal out incomprehensible fire, blows, devastation, and destruction to unbelievers. The idea and reality of God delivering His full and all-powerful wrath back to the sinner for every sin they have ever committed is horrifying to consider.

Finally, hell is described as heavily populated (Matthew 7:13–14). Jesus said that many are on the broad road to destruction and that there are few who find eternal life. Therefore, we can know that there will be many in hell who rejected Christ (Matthew 11:20–24) and neglected Him (Hebrews 2:1–4). Not only that, but there will also be many people that professed to know Christ but were never truly converted; they never came to a saving knowledge of Him. Even worst, there will be a large number of people who were deceived into thinking they belonged to Christ and even made a profession of faith, attended church, sang hymns, gave offerings, owned a Bible, played on a praise team, taught Sunday school, served as a pastor, served as a deacon, and served but never came to a saving faith in Him (Matthew 7:21–23). Hell will be heavily populated with those in false religious systems, with those in false Christian systems, and even those who are in true Bible-believing churches but who never came to a saving knowledge in Christ. Jesus warns us in Matthew 7:14 that, indeed, there are few who find salvation, "*For the gate is narrow and the way is hard that leads to life, and* ***those who find it are few***" (emphasis added).

The soul-sobering reality of hell should cause everyone to test whether they are truly in the faith. When we contemplate the good news, let us always keep the bad news in mind. The bad news heightens the good news of Christ. The bad news should inextricably and unequivocally heighten our love for the Lord. The bad news will multiply a thousandfold the wonder of a verse such as Romans 5:8: "*But God shows his love for us in that while we were still sinners, Christ died for us.*"

The Good News in Scripture

In Romans 1:1–4, Paul writes this regarding the importance of the Scripture and pointing to the person and work of Jesus Christ:

> *Paul, a servant of Christ Jesus, called to be an apostle, set apart for the gospel of God,* ***which he promised beforehand through his prophets in the holy Scriptures****, concerning his Son, who was descended from David according to the flesh and was declared to be the Son of God in power according to the Spirit of holiness by his resurrection from the dead, Jesus Christ our Lord.* (emphasis added)

Here, we see that good news was promised through the prophets in God's Word, and this good news concerned God's Son. In fact, Peter announced this very same truth when he preached at Solomon's Colonnade as recorded in Acts 3:18: "*But what God foretold by the mouth of all the prophets, that his Christ would suffer, he thus fulfilled.*" So, we see that Christ is the fulfillment of what the prophets spoke of regarding the gospel; both Paul and Peter proclaim that Jesus is the fulfillment of what the prophets spoke of in the Old Testament. Though there are many prophecies about Christ in the Old Testament; below are just eight prophecies dealing with the suffering of Christ that have been fulfilled:

- **Genesis 3:15** – Moses wrote that the woman's promised Seed would bruise the head of the serpent and that the serpent would bruise the heel of the Seed; fulfilled on Calvary (Mark 15:16–40, Matthew 26:57–27:50, Luke 22:47–23:49, John 18:1–19:30).
- **Psalm 41:9 and 55:12–14** – The psalmist wrote that Christ would be betrayed by a friend; fulfilled in John 13:18, 21.
- **Zechariah 11:12** – Zechariah wrote that Christ would be sold for thirty pieces of silver in; fulfilled in Matthew 26:15.
- **Zechariah 11:13** – Zechariah wrote that Christ would be given for the price of a potter's field; fulfilled in Matthew 27:7.
- **Psalm 22:14–15** – David wrote that Christ would suffer intensely; fulfilled in Luke 22:42, 44.

- **Isaiah 53:4–12** – Isaiah wrote that Christ would suffer for others; fulfilled in all the gospel accounts of Christ's betrayal, unjust trials, beatings, and crucifixion.
- **Isaiah 53:7** – Isaiah promised that Christ would be patient and silent under suffering in; fulfilled in Matthew 26:63, 27:12–14.
- **Micah 5:1** – Micah wrote that Christ would be struck on the cheek; fulfilled in Matthew 27:30.

It is estimated that the likelihood or mere chance that eight prophecies would be fulfilled in Christ is 10^17. The likelihood that forty-eight prophecies would be fulfilled in Christ carries a mathematical chance of 10^157, which is 157 zeros. One of the many reasons why Scripture is reliable and trustworthy is the fact that God prophesied about future events that have been fulfilled. Therefore, not only do we see the unbelievable foreknowledge and sovereignty of God-fulfilling prophecy, but we also understand how crucial the Holy Scripture is to the gospel and, more specifically as we'll learn, how it declares Jesus Christ. Scripture points to Jesus Christ! The Old Testament predicts Him; the gospels reveal Him; Acts proclaims Him; the epistles explain Him, and Revelation anticipates Him. The gospel rests on the sturdy foundation of the Old Testament, which points to Jesus Christ. Scripture, both the Old and New Testament, is authoritative, inerrant, infallible, and all-sufficient because it is inspired by the God who is all-powerful, all-knowing, and never-changing (2 Timothy 3:16).

The Good News – The Person of the Lord Jesus Christ

> *Paul, a servant of Christ Jesus, called to be an apostle, set apart for the gospel of God, which he promised beforehand through his prophets in the holy Scriptures,* ***concerning his Son, who was descended from David according to the flesh*** *and was declared to be the Son of God in power according to the Spirit of holiness by his resurrection from the dead, Jesus Christ our Lord.* (emphasis added)
>
> —Romans 1:1–4

As we learned from Paul, Scripture points us to the good news of Jesus Christ. The gospel of God is concerned with a person who is God's Son, Jesus Christ. This gospel does not concern the prophet Muhammad of Islam. This gospel does not concern the false god, Allah of Islam. This gospel does not concern Buddha. This gospel does not concern Sun Myung Moon. This gospel does not concern Mary Baker Eddy. This gospel does not concern Ron Hubbard. This gospel does not concern Joseph Smith. This gospel does not concern the false god, Vishnu of Hinduism. This gospel does not concern the false god, Brahman of Hinduism. No, this gospel is all about God's Son, Jesus Christ.

In Romans 1:1–4, notice that Paul claims that Jesus is

the Son of God (verse 3), which is a claim to deity, and then he claims that the Son of God was descended from the physical lineage of David according to the flesh. In this verse, Paul makes a very important Christological statement: He declares that the person of Jesus Christ is both God and man. This Christological truth is an essential component of the gospel.

So, what about the person of Jesus do we need to understand? First, Jesus is God as He is the Son of God (Romans 1:3). Peter makes this great confession in Matthew 16:16 where it says, "*Simon Peter replied, 'You are the Christ, the Son of the living God.'*" Paul makes the same claim to Jesus's deity when he says this about Christ in Colossians 1:19: "*For in him all the fullness of God was pleased to dwell.*" Later, in Colossians 2:9, Paul explains that Jesus Christ is fully God and fully man when he says, "*For in him the whole fullness of deity dwells bodily.*" Likewise, the author of Hebrews says this about Jesus:

> *He is the radiance of the glory of God and the exact imprint of his nature, and he upholds the universe by the word of his power. After making purification for sins, he sat down at the right hand of the Majesty on high.*
>
> —Hebrews 1:3

The author of Hebrews, Paul, Peter, and the Triune God all make the same confession: Jesus Christ is the Son of the living God and truly God and truly man.

Because Jesus is God, He is also coequal and coeternal with God the Father and God the Holy Spirit. In John 5:17–18, after Jesus healed an invalid, Jesus makes a statement about being equal with the Father:

> *But Jesus answered them, "My Father is working until now, and I am working." This was why the Jews were seeking all the more to kill Him, because not only was He breaking the Sabbath,* ***but He was even calling God His own Father, making Himself equal with God*** (emphasis added).

In John 10:30, Jesus makes another statement about being coequal with the Father when He says, "*I and the Father are one.*" Jesus reiterates this same truth when He says this about the work He is doing, "*But if I do them, even though you do not believe me, believe the works, that you may know and understand that* ***the Father is in me and I am in the Father***" (John 10:38, emphasis added). Thus, we see Jesus make the claim that He is equal with the Father, which is a claim to be coequal and coeternal with the God the Father.

Additionally, we are told that Jesus is the only begotten Son of God (John 3:16). The phrase *only begotten* has been translated from *monogenés*, which means one-and-only, one of a kind, or one of a class and the only of its kind. Jesus is the only one of-a-kind Son of God. Jesus is not a created being. We can know that Jesus is not a created being because He is the Son of God, and God is immutable and eternal.

God cannot get better, for if He could get better, He would not be God. God cannot get worse, because if He could get worse, He would be less than God. Jesus is not a created being because God is eternal and immutable. God doesn't become more, and God doesn't become less. God has always, is always, and will always be the Triune God.

The aseity of God also demonstrates that Jesus is God and not a created being. The aseity of God simply refers to the attribute that God is self-sufficient and exists of and from Himself by His own self and self-will. John 1:4 captures the aseity of Christ: "***In him was life***, *and the life was the light of men*" (emphasis added). This is simply stating that all created life came from Christ because He is the source of all life, or rather, He is completely self-sufficient and self-existent in and of Himself and needs nothing. The one who is self-sufficient and self-existent in and of Himself cannot be created because He is eternal and is the origin and source of all life. Therefore, Jesus is the coeternal, coequal, and only begotten Son of God. God the Father, God the Son, and God the Holy Spirit were the Triune God in eternity past and will be the Triune God in eternity future.

The Bible describes the person of Christ in many more ways:

- **The Anointed One of God, or the Christ** – Jesus proclaims to be the fulfillment of Isaiah's prophecy (Luke 4:18–19).

- **The Prophet** – Peter declares that Christ is the Prophet that was foretold in Deuteronomy 18 (Acts 3:21–23).
- **King of Kings and Lord of Lords** – Paul claims that Jesus is the eternal King and Lord of lords when he says, "*He who is the blessed and only Sovereign, the King of kings and the Lord of lords*" (1 Timothy 6:15).
- **The Savior** – The angel declares this about Jesus in Luke 2:11: "*For unto you is born this day in the city of David a Savior, who is Christ the Lord.*"
- **The Eternal High Priest** – The author of Hebrews says that Jesus is the eternal High Priest: "*But he holds his priesthood permanently, because he continues forever. . . . For it was indeed fitting that we should have such a high priest, holy, innocent, unstained, separated from sinners, and exalted above the heavens*" (Hebrews 7:24–26).
- **The Creator and Sustainer of the Universe** – (John 1:1–14, Hebrews 1:1–3, Colossians 1:16–17, 1 Corinthians 8:6).
- **The Son of David** – Jesus was born of the virgin Mary (Matthew 1:23); He was born from the lineage of David and is the Son of David (Matthew 1:1–16, Luke 3:23–38, Psalm 132:11, Jeremiah 23:5, and 2 Samuel 2:8–17, 27–29).

- **The only Mediator between God and man** – (1 Timothy 2:5).
- **The Baptizer with the Holy Spirit** – (Matthew 3:11)

Thus, we understand that Jesus Christ is truly God and man, which is reflected in many descriptions and truths about His person and work.

The Good News – The Work of the Lord Jesus Christ

> *Paul, a servant of Christ Jesus, called to be an apostle, set apart for the gospel of God, which he promised beforehand through his prophets in the holy Scriptures, concerning his Son, who was descended from David according to the flesh* ***and was declared to be the Son of God in power according to the Spirit of holiness by his resurrection from the dead, Jesus Christ our Lord*** (emphasis added).
>
> —Romans 1:1–4

So now that we know about the sinful condition of man, the punishment that man deserves, and the person of the Lord Jesus Christ, we run into a divine dilemma. The divine dilemma is this: How can sinful man be forgiven and reconciled to a just and holy God? How is it possible for God to be a God of justice and punish sin, yet also be the justifier of sinful men? How is it possible for God to punish sinners and yet somehow forgive sinners? Man's sin is incurable. Man cannot earn or merit heaven because sin must be punished. So how can this divine dilemma be solved?

The divine dilemma is solved in the person and work of the Lord Jesus Christ. Christ had to become a man because the wages of sin is death (Romans 6:23), and God cannot die because God is eternal. Therefore, Jesus needed to be a man to die in the place of sinful men. Jesus needed to be a sinless man to take on the curse of the law, suffer divine punishment, and die in man's place (Galatians 3:13, Romans 8:3). The Son of God needed to become the Son of David to die in our place and make the only atonement for man's sin as it says in Romans 8:3:

> *For God* [the Father] *has done what the law, weakened by the flesh, could not do. By sending his own Son in the likeness of sinful flesh and for sin, he* [God the Father] ***condemned sin in the flesh*** [Jesus Christ] (emphasis added).

The Son of God needed to be condemned by His Father on the cross in place of sinful men. The Son of God needed to become the Son of Man to be the mediator between God and man (1 Timothy 2:5). A mediator intervenes to restore peace between two parties. As we saw earlier in this chapter, these two parties were at enmity with each other, and their differences were unreconcilable. The mediator must stand in the middle and be equal to both sides. Jesus had to be truly God to represent God to man, and He needed to be truly man to represent man to God. No one else could have stood between these two parties. No angel or prophet could have mediated between God and man. Only God could take the wrath of God; Only God could live a sinless life.

So, what is this work of Christ that was powerful to save sinners, justify men, and allow God to forgive transgressors? Paul answers this question in Romans 1:4 where he says that Jesus "*was declared the Son of God in power according to the Spirit of holiness by his resurrection from the dead, Jesus Christ our Lord.*" Thus, we see that the resurrection points us to the redeeming work of Christ.

Jesus's teaching and miracles were impossible to ignore. In His teaching He made several claims to deity such as being Lord of the Sabbath (Matthew 12:8), the Good Shepherd (10:11), the only way to the Father (John 14:6), and more. Jesus's miracles and life validated His claim to be God. Jesus also promised that He would be resurrected from the dead, a sign that He was, indeed, the Christ, the Son of the living God. He promised that He would give them the sign of Jonah, which was a predictive prophecy given in picture rather than in word (Matthew 12:38–42, 16:4; Luke 11:29). As Jonah spent three days and three nights in the belly of the great fish, so Jesus spent three days in the heart of the earth. It looked like the end of Jonah, but it wasn't. It looked like the end of Jesus, but it wasn't. Jonah was in the depths of the sea; Jesus was buried in the depths of the earth in the tomb. Jonah came out, and Jesus came out. Jonah was a picture of Jesus's resurrection. Jesus said in John 2:19, "*Destroy this temple, and in three days I will raise it up.*" Again, Jesus was speaking of His death and resurrection. Jesus also reasoned with and taught His disciples that He needed to be killed and raised to life on the third day (Matthew 16:21–22, 17:22–23, 20:17–19; Mark 8:31, 9:30–32, 10:32–34; Luke 9:21–22, 9:43–45, 18:31–34). Jesus also proclaimed that He had power to lay down His life and resurrect himself (John 10:17–18). Therefore, we see that Jesus's resurrection from the dead was and is central to the message of the gospel.

If Jesus could not resurrect Himself, it would prove He was not one with the Father (John 5:17–18). If Jesus could not resurrect Himself, He would be a lying prophet (Matthew 16:21–22, 17:22–23, 20:17–19; Mark 8:31, 9:30– 32, 10:32–34; Luke 9:21–22, 9:43–45, 18:31–34). If Jesus could not resurrect Himself, it would be evidence that He was not the Son with whom the Father was well pleased (Matthew 3:17). If Jesus could not resurrect Himself, it would be evidence that He was not anointed by the Holy Spirit (Luke 4:18–21). However, all of Jesus's works, teaching, and life were validated by His resurrection, which proved that He is the Christ, the Son of the living God. Without the resurrection, Christ's claims and work would have meant nothing. If Jesus had died and not risen, He would not have been the Resurrection and the Life (John 11:25). If Jesus had not risen, He would have been like any other man who dies and does not come back to life (Psalm 90:1–12, Ecclesiastes 7:2). If Jesus had not risen, all His claims and miracles would have amounted to nothing as even Moses and Elisha were able to perform miracles but could not raise themselves from the dead.

Without the resurrection, Jesus's claims and work would have been invalidated. Without the resurrection, Jesus would not be a conqueror over death. Siddhartha Gautama of Buddhism could not resurrect himself from the dead. Kong Qiu of Confucianism could not resurrect himself from the dead. Lao Tzu of Taoism could not resurrect himself from the dead. Joseph Smith of Mormonism could not resurrect himself from the dead. Muhammed of Islam could not resurrect himself from the dead. Mary Baker Eddy of Christian Science could not resurrect herself from the dead. Charles Taze Russell of the Jehovah's Witnesses could not resurrect himself from the dead. If Christ could not resurrect Himself from the dead, Paul would be exactly right about the Christian faith when he says, "*For if the dead are not raised, not even Christ has been raised. And if Christ has not been raised, your faith is futile and you are still in your sins*" (1 Corinthians 15:16–17).

However, Jesus's work on the cross was accepted; His resurrection was proof positive that His salvific work was accepted by God. Christ's resurrection was God's apologetic on the sufficiency of Christ's substitutionary suffering and death on the cross for sinners. The resurrection was God's ultimate validation of Jesus's work on the cross. Jesus raised himself from the dead (John 10:17–18), God the Father raised Jesus from the dead (Galatians 1:1), and the Holy Spirit raised Jesus from the dead (Romans 8:11). All three persons of the Godhead raised Jesus from the dead (Acts 2:24)! God approved of Jesus's atoning and propitiating work by raising Him from the dead.

So, what did Jesus's perfect work secure? In Romans 1:3, Paul spoke of Jesus's deity and humanity. In Romans 1:4, he has fast-forwarded to Christ's resurrection. So, what is Paul trying to do by attesting to Jesus's deity and human birth and then going directly to the resurrection? He is capturing the entire life and work of Christ. Paul is saying that this gospel is about the person of Jesus (Romans 1:3) and the work of Jesus (Romans 1:4). Therefore, an essential component of the gospel includes Jesus's work, which include His teaching, miracles, sinless life, substitutionary atonement, resurrection, ascension, present enthronement, and Second Coming.

So, how is one to understand Jesus's work that was validated by the Resurrection? His work can be summed up in eight words: Propitiation, Reconciliation, Redemption, Expiation, Regeneration, Justification, Glorification, and Domination. For the purposes of this book, we will look at Christ's work of propitiation, which brought about reconciliation, expiation, redemption, glorification, justification, and demonstrated Christ's domination.

The word *propitiation* comes from the word *hilastérion*, which means a sin offering, by which the wrath of the deity is appeased by means of propitiation. As we learned earlier, God hates sin and wickedness. God is angry with the wicked every day. God sees sin as filthy and defiling, as open hostility toward Him, and as an abomination. God considers sin evil and wicked; He simply hates sin with all His being. Therefore, God needed a way to punish sin; He needed a way to propitiate or appease His righteous wrath toward sin and man. If there's anything that can be learned from the Old Testament Levitical system, it is that the sacrifice of goats, calves, bulls, and heifers, ceremonial washings, and grain and fellowship offerings never brought the Jews into the presence of God (Hebrews 9:9–10). Good works never brought the people into the presence of God. However, the God-man, Jesus Christ, is able to act as a mediator between both parties—God and man—who were at enmity with each other. Neither animals nor angels could step in and mediate. Only one person, the Lord Jesus Christ, could be the sinless sacrifice representing man to God and God to man and mediate between the two parties.

Jesus's work required that He fulfill the law and the prophets by living a sinless life and meeting all the requirements of God's law and prophecy (Matthew 3:15, 5:17). In Matthew 22:36–37, Jesus was asked what the greatest commandment was, and He replied, "*You shall love the Lord your God with all your heart and with all your soul and with all your mind.*" Therefore, we know that there was not one millisecond when Christ did not fulfill this commandment perfectly. Christ lived His entire life in full and complete obedience, loving the Lord God with all His heart, soul, mind, and strength. On the other hand, we should see that there's not one millisecond when man has ever perfectly obeyed this command. Jesus lived a perfect and sinless life, and the entirety of His life was one of loving the Lord perfectly with all His heart, soul, mind and strength in complete obedience to God's law. Jesus needed to be sinless to offer Himself as a blameless propitiating sacrifice to please God. If Jesus had sinned, He would not have been a pleasing sacrifice to God. If Jesus had sinned, He would have been like every other man and could not have presented Himself as a blameless, sinless, and undefiled sacrifice for the sins of mankind.

Second Corinthians 5:21 says, "*For our sake he made him to be sin who knew no sin, so that in him we might become the righteousness of God.*" Here Paul speaks of Christ as a sinless offering—living a sinless life. So, what does it mean that Christ was made to be sin? Does it mean that when Christ was on the cross, He became defiled and corrupted? Does it mean that His nature became something vile, loathsome, and sinful? How did Christ become sin?

Before we answer, let's think about how Christ makes sinners righteous when they believe the gospel. The moment a person believes in the gospel and is saved, they do not become a righteous being. That is to say, the moment they believe, they are not so transformed in their nature that they become perfectly righteous and never again sin. We are not infused with a special grace that causes us never to sin. The moment that someone repents and believes in Christ, they are forensically and legally declared righteous before the throne of God. This is a legal declaration before the throne of God in which one is declared righteous not based on one's merits or works, but on the virtue and merit of Jesus Christ, and God treats us as perfectly righteous in Christ.

Therefore, we can understand how God made Christ to be sin. When Jesus Christ was on the cross, His nature did not become polluted. He did not become some vile being. No, what happened was that the sins of His people were imputed or reckoned to Him, and before the throne of God, He was declared guilty, and He was treated by God as a guilty sinner. He always was and will be the spotless Lamb of God. However, on the cross, the sins of His people were imputed to Him. He was legally declared guilty, and then God treated Him as a righteous God should treat the wicked. Upon the cross, the Father treated His Son as the infidel, the sinner, and the lawbreaker.

Galatians 3:13 says that Christ became a curse: "*Christ redeemed us from the curse of the law by becoming a curse for us—for it is written, 'Cursed is everyone who is hanged on a tree.'*" So what does it mean when Jesus became a curse? What is a curse? A curse is the opposite of a blessing. Every curse pronounced in the Bible was to fall on Jesus upon the cross. The divine curse and punishment that is due to sinners in hell, fell upon the beloved Son of God when the Father showed up in judgment and darkness to take His omnipotent, fiery, and vengeful wrath out on His Son (Matthew 27:45–6).

So how did God the Father treat Christ as a cursed sinner? We get a picture of this if we simply look at what it means to be cursed rather than blessed by examining the Beatitudes in Matthew 5:

- Because Christ became a curse, He was punished as one who is refused entrance into the Kingdom of heaven rather than inheriting the kingdom (Matthew 5:3).
- Because Christ became a curse, He was punished and suffered divine wrath rather than comfort (Matthew 5:4).
- Because Christ became a curse, all the goodness of God was taken away, and He suffered and died under the wrath of God as miserable and wretched rather than being satisfied (Matthew 5:6).
- Because Christ became a curse, He received divine justice and punishment rather than divine mercy (Matthew 5:7). He was cut off from God as one bearing disgrace rather than being called a son of God (Matthew 5:9, Psalm 22:1).

Jesus offered Himself up as a sinless offering to God the Father so that God the Father could place all the sins of God's people on Jesus and curse Jesus as if He was the vile sinner. Upon that cross, Jesus suffered the wrath of God for His elect (John 10:11). Those in hell are the only ones who have an idea of what Jesus suffered on the cross and know what it is to be cursed. Leading up to the crucifixion, it wasn't the nails, the flogging, the crown of thorns, the punching, and beatings that Jesus dreaded. Even in the first century, there were Christians who were killed by being hung on a tree and being lit on fire, and they went to their deaths singing hymns of praise to God. Jesus wasn't dreading the physical beatings. No, it was the full cup of wrath and the righteous anger of God toward sin that Jesus dreaded (Matthew 26:39).

Tim Conway has a helpful word on the cup of wrath that Jesus drank down:

> Mark tells us He said on His face, "Abba, Father, if it be possible, let this cup pass from Me if it be possible." Matthew says that Christ spoke to His disciples and He said this, "My soul is very sorrowful, even to death." I want you to think about those words. Do you understand what it meant for a man to be righteous? It meant that death and the law had no claim on Him. He could not die until He was made sin! And yet he says, "I am sorrowful unto death." The NAS says grieved to the point of death. Do you realize what He's saying? Do you realize what death is?! Death is when the soul is ripped apart from the body! Here is Christ understand, He is not under the load of sin! He has not gone to the cross yet! It is only in anticipation of the cross! It is only a thought about what He will endure! And the very thought of it is enough to rip Him soul from body and He is at that very point. Now to the sinner that

> is offensive. . . . You think about that. The God-man Himself in anticipation of the wrath of God is ready to be severed. He is ready to be split. He is ready to be ripped apart with anguish. You let that come into your minds, your hearts, your souls, your thoughts that a righteous man in anticipation of the horrors of the cross should come to such a point.[15]

God didn't unload a rifle firing squad on His Son. God didn't unload a nuclear bomb on His Son. God didn't unload the full heat of the sun on His Son. No, God unloaded something far more terrifying than all those combined. God unloaded His full unbridled, unrestrained, and omnipotent wrath on His only begotten Son; only the eternal Son of God could take the omnipotent wrath from His Father. Only the Son of God could be presented as a sinless propitiation. Only the eternal Son of God could suffer the eternal punishment we deserve.

To get a picture of this wrath, let's imagine a scenario. Let's imagine a father who has only one son whom he deeply loves. The father decides he's going to show his magnanimous love and put it on display by having his son pay the ransom for twenty serial murderers and rapists so they can be set free and forgiven. As part of the ransom to release the twenty criminals, the punishment that is due to the twenty criminals must be paid. So, here's what the father does. The father chooses to pay the punishment for the twenty criminals by taking the punishment out on his one and only beloved son, and the son agrees to take on the punishment of the twenty criminals. The punishment for these twenty criminals is high and costly, and the twenty criminals deserve the most wrathful punishment. Therefore, the father learns to fly a fighter jet and equips the fighter jet with two nuclear bombs. The father also prepares an area for his son to suffer his wrath, and he surrounds his son with one million nuclear bombs and plans to crash the plane into his son. The father prepares all this, but first he lets the twenty criminals slap, punch, mock and beat his son until the son's face is no longer recognizable. He then lets the criminals strap his only son whom he loves to the tree surrounded by one million nuclear bombs. The Father then flies the fighter jet directly at his only beloved son, puts the jet on autopilot, and evacuates the plane while it is headed for his son. The jet then crashes into his son; the son is crushed by the plane, and the fire is unleashed by the nuclear bombs consumes his son. The father then turns his face away in disapproval from his only son and cannot bear to look at his son as he unleashes upon his son the punishment that was due to the twenty criminal serial murders and rapists. The father crushes and curses his only beloved son and is satisfied.

This example falls woefully and pathetically short of describing the wrath of God that was poured out on Christ. God's wrath is far greater and far more terrible than we can imagine. The temperature of a 1-megaton nuclear weapon can produce temperatures of about 100 million degrees Celsius at its center, which is about four to five times hotter than the sun's core. Even in this example, we fall woefully short of the omnipotent fiery wrath of God on sinners. The wrath of God that was taken out on Christ was the propitiation and satisfaction that paid for man's sin. Christ, the sacrificial Lamb bore the sins and punishment of His elect on the cross (Isaiah 53). Therefore, we should never forget and always seek to fathom the incomprehensible worth of Jesus Christ's substitutionary work on the cross for sinners. Not only did He suffer the wrath of God for one man, but He has also suffered the wrath of God for the sins of a great multitude of humanity (Revelation 7:9). Romans 8:1 says, "*There is therefore now no condemnation for those who are in Christ Jesus.*" There is no condemnation for those in Christ Jesus because Christ paid the condemnation and punishment for sinners. Every drop of wrath for those whom the Son of God died was satisfied and placated at Calvary. There is not one drop of wrath left for those in Christ Jesus. The wrathful cannon of God has been unloaded and emptied on the Son of God who loved us and gave Himself up for us (Galatians 2:20). Again, Tim Conway has a helpful word on the unfathomable horrors of Christ being condemned and forsaken on the cross:

> Jesus cried out with a loud voice, "My God, my God, why have you forsaken me?" God forsaken! That is what Jesus was on the cross. He was God forsaken. Don't use that terminology flippantly! He was God forsaken. The Son was forsaken. What can you say? God the Father forsook God the Son. Something in

that sounds like what it cost to redeem man shook the very foundations of the Trinity itself. And I don't have words. I can't tell you. I can't go there. I don't know. Who can explain it?

Brethren, I had a guy call me this week. Again, it was another man struggling with being saved. He said, "I am at the end of myself. I am a great sinner. I have done many wicked things in my life. I have sinned for no other reason than just to sin. I am at the end of myself." He said, "But I think I am too great a sinner to be saved." I said, "Sir, you may think that is a humble statement." But I said, "That is a statement of such wickedness and pride you have no idea." I said, "Sir, have you ever looked at the cross? Have you ever seen the Son of God forsaken, His soul spilled, crushed under the almighty affliction of His Father? Have you ever beheld that? Have you ever beheld him in the garden just as in anticipation of what was going to come . . . pleading with His Father? Are you going to look at that and say that isn't sufficient for your sin? What are you making that out to be? That was no trivial thing." Christ going to the cross was not a waltz through the garden, folks. What he endured there you and I will never know. The only ones that can come closest to knowing it is that soul that after 10 billion ages has drank [sic] the cup of God's wrath and will have to do for forever more because he will never get close to the point of knowing fully what it

> was Christ endured. . . . No man has the capacity to take away the full guilt of sin or any of the guilt of sin! What does a man think he's saying when he says, "I think I'm too wicked?" Do you think Jesus Christ came into this world and went to the cross to save good people?! Do you think he had his soul spilled to save good people?![16]

When Christ had suffered the wrath of God and was about to yield up His spirit on the cross, He said, "*It is finished*" (John 19:30). The phrase *It is finished*, is translated from *tetelestai*, which means "to end," "to bring to conclusion," "to accomplish," "to fulfill," or "to finish." Note that Jesus didn't say, "I am finished." No! He said, "*It is finished.*" His perfect propitiating and sin-bearing substitutionary work was complete. Jesus paid the full price and penalty for sin. Jesus took the whole wrath of God. There is not one sin of God's people that was not punished at Calvary. There is not one sin of God's people that the Father did not lay on His only begotten Son. God's justice was fully satisfied. In the secular sense, *tetelestai* was used to signify the full payment of a debt. The parchment on which the debt was recorded was stamped with the word *tetelestai*, which meant the debt had been paid in full. Charles Spurgeon shares these insights about this word:

> An ocean of meaning in a drop of language, a mere drop. It would need all the other words that ever were spoken, or ever can be spoken, to explain this

> one word. It is altogether immeasurable. It is high; I cannot attain to it. It is deep; I cannot fathom it. It is finished is the most charming note in all of Calvary's music. The fire has passed upon the Lamb. He has borne the whole wrath that was due to His people. This is the royal dish of the feast of love.[17]

A. W. Pink said of *tetelestai*, "Eternity will be needed to make manifest all that *tetelestai* contains."[18] A. C. Gaebelein said of *tetelestai,* "Never before and never after was ever spoken one word which contains and means so much. It is the shout of the mighty Victor. And who can measure the depths of this one word!"[19]

This is the propitiation that brought reconciliation between God and men (Romans 5:10–11). This is the propitiation that brought about expiation or the forgiveness of sins (Ephesians 1:7, Hebrews 8:12). This is the propitiation that paid the price of redemption (Galatians 3:13). This is the propitiation that brought justification or rather, for God to be the just and justifier of men (Romans 3:26). This is the propitiation, which showed forth God's domination over sin, death, and the devil (Colossians 2:13–15). This is the propitiation that brought about glorification for sinners and glorified the attributes and character of God (1 Corinthians 1:18–25).

Not only does Jesus's work include His resurrection, but it also includes His ascension (24:51) and His second coming and judgment (Revelation 22:12–13, Matthew 25:31–46).

This is the work of the Lord Jesus Christ, which secured eternal life and salvation for men. The divine dilemma has been solved through the work of Christ.

What great news this is from Heaven! Jesus needed to be born of a virgin (Matthew 1:23), so we could be born of God (John 3:3, 7). Jesus needed to be born a man (Matthew 1:23), so we could be born again (John 3:3, 7). Jesus needed to be the Son of Man (Luke 19:10), so that we could be sons of God (1 John 3:1). Jesus needed to be rejected by God (Isaiah 53:3), so we could be resurrected by God (1 Corinthians 15:52). Jesus needed to be despised (Isaiah 53:3), so we would not be damned (Romans 1:18–32). Jesus needed to be crushed by God (Isaiah 53:5, 10), so we would not be cursed by God (Galatians 3:13). Jesus needed to be crucified (Isaiah 53:5), so we could be justified (Romans 3:24). Jesus needed to be forsaken (Matthew 27:46), so we could be forgiven (Isaiah 53:12). Jesus suffered (Isaiah 53:11), so we would be saved (Matthew 1:23). Jesus needed to suffer the wrath of God (Isaiah 53:10), so He could show forth the riches of God (Ephesians 2:7). Jesus needed to be resurrected (Isaiah 53:11), so we could be perfected (Hebrews 10:14). Jesus needed to bear reproach (Hebrews 13:13), so we could be redeemed (Romans 3:24). Jesus offered himself as a sacrifice (Hebrews 9:26), so we could be saints (2 Corinthians 5:21).

God did this all because of the great love with which He loved His own (Ephesians 2:4)!

Man's Responsibility to Respond to the Lord Jesus Christ in Repentance and Faith

> *Through whom we have received grace and apostleship to bring about the* ***obedience of faith*** *for the sake of his name among all the nations* (emphasis added).
>
> —Romans 1:5

As we consider this last component of the gospel, we will perform a brief exposition of Matthew 16:24–26 to understand repentance and saving faith. Why would we transition to this text of Scripture in Matthew 16:24–26? The Lord often gave gospel invitations to come to and follow Him in a saving way. Today in Christianity, repentance and true faith are watered down. Repentance can be stripped down to be a liturgical confession and absolution, saying the sinner's prayer, or simply asking for forgiveness. Likewise, saving faith can be stripped down to having an intellectual knowledge of some of the facts about Christ, believing the Apostle's Creed, believing the Three Forms of Unity, and many other spurious and man-made definitions of faith. Not only that, but many churches such as the Roman Catholic church, Eastern Orthodox church, Lutheran church, United Methodist church, Episcopal church, Churches of Christ teach sacramental salvation by water baptism. Whether a church teaches salvation by sacramentalism, works, or strips the meaning out of repentance and faith, we need to rightly define true repentance and saving faith. There is also a pernicious doctrine of presumptive regeneration in reformed churches which can go as far as teaching that all children that are members of believing parents are presumed to be regenerate until evidence demonstrates otherwise. Therefore, we will exposit one of Christ's clearest gospel calls to repentance and faith in Matthew 16:24–26. Before we begin our exposition, consider these words by Tim Conway regarding the gospel call of repentance and faith:

> You see what we're doing is we're coming in and we're pressing people. Lay down the weapons of your rebellion. Change your mind about how important Christ is and what He did on that cross. Cry out to Him in desperation because you're in peril! You better flee from the wrath of God! You better save yourselves from this wicked generation and you better do it right now because I cannot guarantee you that you have life and breath tomorrow and you're living right now for your sins and you're living for all these things, but you've got to know that there's an eternal night coming for those who die enemies of this Christ and He is serious! He's no babe in a manger anymore. He is now a judge and He is going to judge you and you've got to stand before the judgment seat of Christ and you can't get away from it no matter how badly you want to get away from it, and it's coming and it's soon going to be here.
>
> Brethren, we don't want to come away with this man-made way of letting sinners off the hook. . . . Don't

> leave them with any hope! If the only way to leave an unrepentant sinner with hope is to bring the standard down by telling them to pray, better off to leave them without hope. Leave them with no hope other than **repenting and believing** immediately. No other hope! None! Don't tell them to pray. Don't give them some off way to make them feel OK while they continue in rebellion against Jesus Christ. Don't do that. Don't do that! Your message as ambassadors of Christ is to tell sinners to be reconciled to God. . . . You press them to turn at once. . . . Brethren, if we would win souls, this is what we want to do. We want to press people to **repent**. We want to press people to **believe** in the Lord Jesus Christ (emphasis added).[20]

> *Then Jesus told his disciples, "If anyone would come after me, let him deny himself and take up his cross and follow me."*
>
> —Matthew 16:24

In this section, we are going to see the Lord issue a gospel call to follow Him in saving faith. Christ has explained that the church would be built on Him, the church would be given the keys of the kingdom of heaven, that He needed to die and rise again, and that He and His church would be in conflict with Satan. He will now turn and issue a gospel call. Your response to this gospel call determines whether you save your soul or lose your soul and whether your sins are bound or loosed. Your response to this gospel call determines whether you are inside or outside the kingdom of heaven. This gospel call explains how to pass through the narrow gate; therefore, it is critical to understand this gospel call.

Jesus never hid the cost of what it meant to be one of His disciples or what it meant to believe in Him. The crowd that had gathered with Jesus were made up of true disciples who had left everything to follow Him (Matthew 4:19). One of Jesus's twelve disciples, Judas, followed Him but was unregenerate and unconverted (John 6:70). Some of the people in the crowd were amazed at His teaching but uncommitted (Luke 4:32). Some followed Him because of His miracles but were uncommitted (John 6:2) Some followed Him because He provided food for them but were uncommitted (John 6:26–27). The crowd that followed Jesus was mixed with the committed, the curious, and the counterfeit; it was mixed with the faithful, the feigned, and the false. The crowd that followed Jesus was mixed with the sincere, the skeptical, and the pseudo.

The crowd and religious leaders were faced with deciding what to do with Jesus based on His claims and the works He was doing (John 5:36). There were obstacles to following Jesus; His teaching caused many of His disciples to depart from Him (John 6:66). Jesus told the religious Jews that they were poor, blind, prisoners, and oppressed, and this message caused them to want to kill Him (Luke 4:19–29). Jesus's healing on the Sabbath caused the religious leaders to want to kill Him (Mark 3:6). Jesus's claim to deity caused people and religious leaders to stumble (Luke 5:21–25). Jesus's claim to be one with God the Father caused the Jewish leaders to want to kill Him (John 5:16–18). Jesus healing the demoniac and casting out demons into pigs caused great fear in an entire city, and they asked Him to leave (Luke 8:37). Each person had to make a decision about how to respond to the person and work of the Lord Jesus Christ.

Notice that Christ's invitation to follow Him is for everyone. Christ's call to follow Him in a salvific way was and is open to everyone. Christ would turn to both His disciples and to the crowd when He issued the call. Jesus didn't hide this invitation in the fine print. Jesus didn't whisper this call. Jesus didn't issue this call to only a select few. No, Jesus Christ invited all people everywhere to follow Him. To committed followers, this was a reminder of the call they had answered and an exhortation to follow Him with deep commitment. For those who were unconvinced, undecided, and opposed, this served as a clarion call to come and follow Christ in a salvific way. This invitation rang out to the crowds 2,000 years ago, and the invitation remains open to all people everywhere today.

Notice also that the one who issues the call also defines the terms of how He will be followed. Mankind can only follow Jesus Christ on His terms. There are no escape clauses. There is no bargaining or negotiating with the terms. Jesus is the one who defines the terms of what it means to be His disciple, to be a believer, to be His slave. Jesus is the one who defines how to enter the narrow gate (Matthew 7:13–14). Jesus is the one who defines how to enter the kingdom of God (Mark 1:15). Jesus is the one who defines how to enter the kingdom of heaven (Matthew 4:17). This is the call that the Lord Jesus Christ has put forth; you either accept this call or deny this call. You can embrace the call or ignore the call, but how you respond to this call determines all eternity for you. How you respond to this call determines whether you lose your soul or keep your soul.

Jesus knew that all types of people would desire to come to Him in a salvific way. The word "*wants*" comes from *theló*, which means to wish, desire, intend, or to be willing. *Theló* carries with it the desire, wish, or intention to follow a course of action. Jesus knew that the religious Jew, the down-and-out prostitute, the despised tax collector, the desperate leper, the half-breed Samaritan, the detested Gentile, the desolate paralytic, the religious teacher, the religious leader, and others would desire to receive salvation from Him. Likewise, even today, Jesus knows that the religious Roman Catholic bishop, the religious Lutheran, the religious Eastern Orthodox churchgoer, the opioid addict, the porn addict, the self-righteous professing Christian, the practicing homosexual, the crooked businessman, the moral but lost grandparent, and many other people would desire salvation through Him. Jesus wasn't looking for a large number of disciples. Jesus was looking for the quality of the disciple. Additionally, the phrase *to come* is written in the aorist tense and infinitive mood. This is calling for a simple, single momentary action. Another way of saying this would be to say, "If anyone would desire to come to me once and for all, let him deny himself, take up his cross, and follow me." For all those desiring to come after Him in a salvific way, Jesus wanted everyone to be crystal clear on what it meant to be a believer, a disciple, and a follower of Him. Jesus didn't want people to be self-deceived. Jesus didn't want people to be misguided followers. Therefore, for all people who seek to be His followers and even those that would reject Him, He issued this call.

Repentance

In Matthew 16:24, the first command He gives to the crowd is to "*deny himself*," which is given in the aorist tense and imperative mood. The word *deny* comes from the original word *aparneomai*, which is a compound word comprised of *apó* meaning "from" and *arnéomai* meaning "deny." The prefix *apó* intensifies *arnéomai*, and the word *aparneomai* means to strongly deny or to utterly deny. It is important to note that this verb is in aorist tense and imperative mood, which simply means that it is a command, which signifies and calls for a one-time activity or the completion of an activity. Unlike a verb, which is a present imperative, meaning the action is commanded to be followed in the present tense, the aorist imperative calls for the completion of the action. Therefore, we can know that Jesus is calling for a decisive self-denial for anyone that would desire to be His disciple.

Jesus used this word, *aparnéomai*, when prophesying Peter's denial of Him. Peter's first denial of Jesus was in front of a servant girl who said to Peter in Matthew 26:69, "*You too were with Jesus the Galilean,*" and Peter responded to her in Matthew 26:70, "*I do not know what you are talking about*" (NASB). Peter's second denial took place with another slave woman who saw Peter and said to him in Matthew 26:71, "*This man was with Jesus of Nazareth*" (NASB), and Peter took an oath and responded in Matthew 26:72 by saying, "*I do not know the man*" (NASB). Peter's third denial came when he was approached by some where they said in Matthew 26:73, "*You really are one of them as well, since even the way you talk gives you away*" (NASB), and Peter cursed and swore and said to them in Matthew 26:74, "I do not know the Man" (NASB)! In these verses, we get an idea of how strong this word, *aparneomai,* is in terms of denying and refusing association with someone.

So, what does it mean when Jesus called for self-denial? In Jesus's ministry, He was very clear about what was included with self-denial. Jesus would call for a self-denial of:

- Self-righteousness (Luke 18:9–14)
- Works-righteousness salvation (Matthew 5:20)
- The love of money (Matthew 6:24)
- False religion (Matthew 15:12–14)
- Following the world and the deceitfulness of wealth (Matthew 13:22)

- Loving the world (John 15:19)
- Living for worldly comfort (Luke 9:57–58)
- Other relationships taking preeminence over Him (Luke 14:26, Matthew 10:34–38)
- Running one's own life (Luke 14:26)

Jesus called for a self-denial and repentance of one's sin. Jesus's call to deny oneself is a radical call of repentance, submission, and faith in Him. Just as Peter said, "*I do not know the man*," so all true believers in Christ are called to say the same thing to our sinful, self-righteous, self-willed, and self-absorbed way of life. This is a call to be done living for yourself. It was a call to stop being the lord of your life. Jesus is calling you to deny the unholy trinity of me, myself, and I. This is a call to repent of your sins, say goodbye to your worldly desires and pride, say goodbye to self-will, self-sufficiency, self-wishes, and self-righteousness in exchange for the Lord Jesus Christ's yoke, His will, and His rule over your life. Jesus called for a submission unto Him by saying goodbye to one's life.

John the Baptist talked about self-denial and repentance another way. In Luke 3:4–6, John the Baptist said this regarding repentance:

> As it is written in the book of the words of Isaiah the prophet, "The voice of one calling in the wilderness: 'Prepare the way for the Lord, **make his paths straight**. **Every valley shall be filled**, and **every**

> **mountain and hill made low, and the crooked shall become straight**, and **the rough places shall become level ways** and all flesh shall see the salvation of God'" (emphasis added).

John was proclaiming that every person needed to clean out their spiritual closet. He was saying that everyone in Israel needed to get rid of their apathy, pride, distractions, false religion, get other priorities that interfere with God, self-reliance, hypocrisy, self-will, and anything that would prevent them from accepting the Messiah.

He says that the crooked roads shall become straight and the rough ways smooth. Once again, John wasn't calling for a road construction project; he was calling for a total self-evaluation. In verse 5, he says, "*Every valley shall be filled in, every mountain and hill made low.*" When John said that "*every valley shall be filled in,*" he meant that every sin shall be brought up and openly confessed. He was calling the people to confess their sins and not hold anything back. All the debase sins that the people indulged in and cherished were to be raised up and elevated so that you could be brought low and humbled to receive the Messiah. Notice that he says "every." This was a radical repentance. He was saying that the sins that the people knew about in their lives needed to be confessed and rejected. He was saying that all the hidden sins in the valley of one's heart needed to be exposed. Likewise, John said that "every mountain and hill needed to be brought low." This means that every righteous act and every self-exalting accomplishment must be brought low. There was no room for confidence in circumcision. There was no room for confidence in ceremonial washing. There was no room for confidence in Sabbath observance-keeping. He's saying that your sins must be elevated, all your good deeds and religious accomplishments brought low, and every other obstacle in your life must be dealt with and removed. There was no room for religious exaltation, only room for soul-searching repentance and humility and a heart ready to accept the Messiah as Lord and Savior.

Additionally, notice the violent picture of repentance that John paints when he says, "every mountain and hill made low." What would it take to make a mountain low? What type of force and power would it take to make a mountain level with the ground? The undeniable answer is that it would take an earth-shattering crushing force and power to demolish a mountain to bring it low. This is the powerful picture of someone taking a divine sledgehammer and crushing their pride and religious accomplishments.

True repentance does not result in churchgoing religious people relying on their religious works such as, "I've been a Christian all my life," "I've taught Sunday school for thirty years," "I've been an elder and deacon in my church," "I read a devotional five days a week," "I play the organ and am in the worship team," or any of the like. Such self-righteous exaltation is an abomination before God (Luke 18:9–13). True repentance means that a person does not exalt their religious achievement, but confesses their spiritual bankruptcy like Peter who said, "*Depart from me, for I am a sinful man, O Lord*" (Luke 5:8), or the Centurion who said "*I am not worthy to have you come under my roof*" (Luke 7:6), or the tax collector in Christ's parable who said "*God be merciful to me, the sinner*" (Luke 18:13 NASB). When a person truly repents, they see their sin (e.g., adultery, a covetous and wicked heart, religious hypocrisy, idolatry, self-righteousness, or pride), and they hold their sin up high and turn to the Lamb of God who takes away the sin of the world, turn from their sin, and obediently trust and submit to Him (John 1:29).

True self-denial and repentance encompass the whole of one's person—one's mind, heart, will, soul, and body. Every single element of one's person is included in "deny himself" or "deny yourself." In Hebrew, the heart is the center of one's being. It is not merely the home of one's affections, but also the seat of the will and moral purpose. The condition of one's heart determined one's influence. In Proverbs 4:23, we are told to "*watch over your heart with all diligence, for from it flow the springs of life*" (NASB). Jesus warned that true defilement comes from the heart in Matthew 15:18–19, where He said:

> *But the things that come out of the mouth come from the heart, and those things defile the person. For out of the heart come evil thoughts, murders, acts of adultery, other immoral sexual acts, thefts, false testimonies, and slanderous statements* (NASB).

A follower of Christ is to deny the whole of oneself. In fact, Jesus clarifies this in Matthew 16:25–26:

> *For whoever wants to save his* ***life*** *will lose it; but whoever loses his* ***life*** *for my sake will find it. For what good will it do a person if he gains the whole world, but forfeits his* ***soul****? Or what will a person give in exchange for his* ***soul*** (NASB, emphasis added)?

The words *life* and *soul* come from the original word *psuché, which* can mean the human soul, the soul as the seat of affections and will, the self, a human person, an individual, or a life. It is a person's distinct identity. Jesus was calling for the whole of one's body and soul to be submitted to Him. No longer would one's personal knowledge and wisdom be the driving force, but rather, it would be replaced with the knowledge and wisdom of the Lord Jesus Christ. Christ is not calling for sinless perfection. May it never be! What Christ is calling for is the renunciation, denunciation, and repudiation of one's life. Jesus is calling for commitment, submission, devotion, dedication, faithfulness, fidelity, and loyalty of one's life unto Him. It is a self-denial that will not learn, think, and act apart from God's Word but will learn, think, and act on sin, salvation, Jesus Christ, the Bible, theology, the church, living, marriage, money, family, job, eternity, and everything else according to God's Word. The self-denying Christian must learn to say yes to Jesus's commands.

In Luke 14:26, Jesus talks about self-denial this way: "*If anyone comes to me and does not* ***hate*** *his own father and* *mother and wife and children and brothers and sisters, yes,* ***and even his own life****, he cannot be my disciple*" (emphasis added). In this verse hating your own life is denying yourself. Additionally, Jesus says that you must not only hate your own life or rather, deny yourself, He says that you must hate those in your closest concentric circle. Of course, this is not talking about hating one's own wife, children, and family members. Jesus is speaking about loving Him more than your own life and anything and everything else. To deny yourself is to love the Lord Jesus Christ above anything and everything else. If you come to Him for salvation and love anyone or any idol more than Him, you cannot be His disciple.

Saving Faith

Notice that Matthew 16:24 includes a second command stating that anyone who wishes to follow Christ must "*take up his cross.*" The word *take up* is also written in the aorist imperative, simply meaning that it is a command that signifies and calls for a one-time activity or the completion of an activity. This is a command to make a final decision to not only deny yourself, but to also die to yourself. Notice that this is not cross-wearing; it is cross-bearing. Bearing a cross 2,000 years ago had a very specific meaning. *Bearing a cross* meant strapping an instrument of death on your back. It was a walk of death that included disgrace, shame, pain, and persecution. Disgrace was guaranteed. Shame was promised. Pain was certain. Persecution was inevitable. Jesus was calling for a self-denying, cross-bearing, Christ-identifying walk of life where a person would so identify with Him that they would do so even to the point of death. In Luke's account, he emphasizes that Christ says this cross-bearing would be daily (Luke 9:23). A cross-bearing death to self was to be the walk and manner of one's life. Cross-bearing was not glorious. In fact, the Jews would have been very familiar with this picture as the Proconsul Varus crucified 2,000 Jews who besieged Sabinus and made an example of them and their insurrection.

Crucifixion to the point of death on the cross could take from six hours to several days and could be due to the after effects of compulsory scourging, maiming, hemorrhaging, and dehydration causing hypovolemic shock. Death could also be precipitated by cardiac arrest. The Roman guards would not leave the site until the victim was dead. They could kill the victim by breaking the victim's legs, stabbing the heart or chest with spears, or building a fire at the foot of the cross to asphyxiate the victim. Therefore, Jesus's command would have been shocking. As we noted earlier, just as one was to deny the unholy trinity of me, myself, and I, they were also called to repent and die to worldly desires, pride, self-will, self-sufficiency, self-wishes, and self-righteousness. They were to live for Christ's yoke, will, and rule over their life. This is a step of self-humiliation. This is a step of self-renunciation. Taking up one's cross is to die to self and surrender and submit to the King of heaven, the Lord Jesus Christ. What does this cross-bearing look like? We see in Foxe's Book of Martyrs, the testimony of believers who denied themselves and took up their cross at their conversion and even to the point of death:

- In the persecutions in the Valleys of Piedmont in the seventeenth century, seven people had their mouths stuffed with gunpowder, which being set fire to, their heads were blown to pieces.[21]
- Jacob Michelino, the chief elder of the church of Bobbio, and several other protestants, were hung on hooks which were fixed in their bellies and were left to die in the most excruciating tortures.[22]
- Paul Garnier, a protestant, had his eyes put out, was then flayed alive, was divided into four parts and his four parts were placed on four principal houses of Lucerne.[23]
- Francis Gros, the son of a clergyman, had his flesh slowly cut from his body into small pieces, and put into a dish before him; two of his children were minced before his sight; and his wife was fastened to a post to witness these cruelties. When the tormentors tired of tormenting the family, they cut off the heads of Francis and his wife and gave the flesh of the whole family to the dogs.[24]
- Rawlins White was put in prison for suspected heresy. Bishop Llandaff tried to persuade Rawlins to recant and revoke the faith but was unable to

> do so. When Rawlins was brought to the stake, the Romish doctrines of the Sacraments was read to Rawlins and he cried out, "Ah! Thou wicked hypocrite, dost thou presume to prove thy false doctrine by Scripture? Look in the text that followeth; did not Christ say, 'Do this in remembrance of me?'" The crowd cried for Rawlins to be set on fire. Rawlins was set on fire, and he received the crown of eternal life.[25]

This is what it means to take up one's cross. It is the initial step of repentance and faith in the Lord Jesus Christ where one will deny themselves and will wholly and preeminently love, repent, submit, and trust in the Lord Jesus Christ even to the point of death (Revelation 2:10). Thus, saving faith is a preeminent loving, submissive, obedient, and repentant faith in the Lord Jesus Christ.

Jesus's third command in Matthew 16:24 is to "*follow me*." The word *follow* comes from *akoloutheó*, which means to follow the one who precedes, to join one as an attendant, or to accompany one. This means to be in the same way with; it carries the idea of cleaving steadfastly to one and conforming wholly to that person's example in living and, if need be, in dying. It is a strong word that gives the idea that the one following is not following begrudgingly but is willingly following step for step with Christ. The one following isn't resentfully following, but rather, is seeking to follow Christ wholeheartedly. The self-denying, cross-bearing follower is conforming their mind to that of Christ to mimic Him in thought, word, deed, and intent.

Unlike the previous two commands, which were in the aorist imperative, this command is in the present imperative. The present imperative signifies that it is a command that is to be continually followed. Jesus is defining the call to submissive saving faith and make the conclusive decision to deny yourself, die to yourself, and to follow Christ wherever He goes as a self-denying, cross-bearing follower. You cannot follow Christ without denying yourself. You cannot follow Christ without taking up your own cross. You cannot change Christ's terms. You cannot wipe away these verses. You cannot bargain with the Way, the Truth, and the Life (John 14:6). Heaven and earth will pass away, but Christ's Word will not pass away (Matthew 5:18, 1 Peter 1:24–25).

Jesus gave several examples in which following Him was connected with hearing and doing. Jesus was very clear on the importance of submissive listening and following, or rather, a submissive faith. In John 10:3–4, Jesus explained that His sheep would be those who listened and followed Him:

> *To him the gate keeper opens. The sheep* ***hear*** *his voice, and he calls his own sheep by name and leads them out. When he was brought out all his own, he goes before them, and the sheep* ***follow*** *him, for they know his voice* (emphasis added).

Likewise, Jesus made a similar statement about a grain of wheat needing to die before it bore fruit, that one must lose one's life to save it, and that His servants would be His faithful followers as He says in John 12:24–26:

> *Truly, truly, I say to you, unless a grain of wheat falls into the earth and dies, it remains alone; but if it dies, it bears much fruit. Whoever loves his life loses it, and whoever hates his life in this world will keep it for eternal life. If anyone serves me, he must* ***follow*** *me; and where I am, there my servant will be also; if anyone serves me, the Father will honor him* (emphasis added).

Jesus adds that the one who hears His words and does them is a wise man whereas those who hear His Word and don't act upon them are foolish (Matthew 7:24–27). Jesus said that those who hear His Word and keep it are blessed: "*Blessed rather are those who* ***hear*** *the word of God and* ***keep it***" (Luke 11:28, emphasis added)! When Jesus called all people to follow Him in a salvific way, it was a call to submissive, self-denying, cross-bearing, and obedient faith. When Jesus stops, His sheep would stop. When Jesus would turn left, His sheep would turn left. Jesus's sheep would learn to think of prayer according to Jesus (Matthew 6:5–15, Luke 18:1–18). Jesus's sheep would learn to think of sin according to Jesus (Matthew 5:21–22, 27–30). Jesus's sheep would learn how to think about His teaching (John 8:31). Jesus's sheep would learn how to live in a fallen world (Matthew 5:13–16). Jesus's sheep would learn how to think of Him (Matthew 12:8, 16:16; Luke 24:46–47; John 6:35, 48, 51; 8:12, 58; 9:5; 10:7, 9, 11, 14; 11:25; 15:1). Jesus's sheep would learn to think of marriage according to Him (Matthew 19:1–10). Jesus's sheep would learn to think of handling persecution according to Him (Matthew 10:16–25). Jesus's sheep would learn how to forgive according to Him (Matthew 18:21–35). This is all to say that Jesus was calling for a self-denying, submissive faith in Him that would willingly follow Him wherever He went.

Another way to describe a self-denying, cross-bearing follower of Christ can be seen in the way that the New Testament authors identified themselves. Many of them identified themselves as a *doulos* or slave. The title of being a slave has negative connotations now, but this word doesn't carry that stigma when it comes to being a slave of Christ in the New Testament. A *doulos* in the New Testament as used by Peter and Paul, was one who willingly committed himself to serve a master he loves and respects. The *doulos* had no life of his own, no will of his own, no purpose of his own, and no plan of his own. All things were subject to his master. Every thought, breath, and effort were subject to the will of his master. The *doulos* was one who was absolutely surrendered and totally devoted to his master. The existence of the *doulos* was for the will and purpose of his master and nothing else.

Paul referred to himself as a slave or *doulos* of Christ (Romans 1:1, Philippians 1:1, Titus 1:1). Paul referred to Timothy as a *doulos* of Christ (Philippians 1:1). James referred to himself as a *doulos* of Christ even though he was half-brother to Jesus (James 1:1). Peter referred to himself as a *doulos* of Christ (2 Peter 2:1). Jude referred to himself as a *doulos* of Christ even though he was half-brother to Jesus (Jude 1:1). John referred to himself as a *doulos* of Christ (Revelation 1:1). Jesus referred to a true believer who did His will as His faithful *doulos* (Matthew 25:21). Jesus said that those who were a true *doulos* of His would do the things He commanded (Luke 17:10). You are either a *doulos* to sin or a *doulos of Christ* (John 8:34–42).

Conversely, the one who claimed allegiance to Christ but never did His work was a wicked and lazy *doulos* (Matthew 25:26). The one who claimed allegiance to Christ but never denied self, bore a cross, and followed Him was self-deceived (Matthew 7:21–23). Even though many people claimed to do works in Christ's name, Jesus said that these many people were never saved, regenerated, or converted into His kingdom. In fact, in Matthew 7:23 He says that He never knew them; the word *never* comes from *oudepote* with *oude* meaning not and *pote* meaning at one time or other. Essentially, when Jesus says, "I never knew you," He is saying that there was never a time when He savingly knew these false hypocritical Christians who claimed allegiance to Him though they claimed allegiance to Him and appeared to be religious. These people were self-deceived and never denied themselves, took up a cross, and came to saving knowledge in Christ.

In speaking of a true believer in Christ, a *doulos*, please note that the true believer has no rights. The true believer has no vote. Jesus becomes the exclusive Lord of the believer's life. Jesus is not following the believer. Jesus is not the copilot of the true believer's life. Jesus is not sitting in the back seat and following where you go. No, at salvation, the believer denies self, dies to self, and takes the leap of saving faith to follow Christ. The believer does not know where the Lord will lead, but the believer will obediently and submissively follow the Lord regardless of where He leads them. That person is not following the world, the flesh, family, friends, or their own understanding. They are following Lord Jesus Christ. Concerning the call to salvation, Charles Spurgeon said, "There are no crown-wearers in heaven that were not cross-bearers here below."[26]

> *For whoever wants to save his life will lose it; but whoever loses his life for my sake will find it.*
>
> —Matthew 16:25

Here in Matthew 16:26, Jesus gives his listeners the ultimate paradox: If you would hold on to your life, you will lose it. That is, if you hold on to your priorities, your own purpose, your personal agenda, false religion, and continue to be lord of your life, then you will lose your life eternally. However, if you will lose your life for the sake of the Lord Jesus Christ and the gospel, you will save it. This is the paradox. You must lose your life to gain it. You must die to live. It is important to notice that the word *life* is translated from *psuché*, which can also be translated as the soul. As we learned earlier, the soul is the home of one's affections and the seat of the will and moral purpose. Is the Lord Jesus Christ worth denying yourself, dying to yourself, and following Him, or is it worth more to remain the lord over your life? There must be a crucifixion before there is a resurrection. You cannot serve two masters as you will ultimately love one and hate the other (Matthew 6:24). You are either with Jesus or you are against Him (Luke 11:23). You either gather with Jesus or you scatter (Matthew 12:30). There are no fence straddlers. There are only those for Christ and those opposed to Christ.

Notice that the one who loses his life, or rather his soul, for Christ's sake and the gospel will save it. Whoever denies the self, takes up their cross, and decides to follow the biblical Jesus will find their life, or rather, eternal life. Eternal life is not just speaking of the quantity of life, meaning eternality. It is also speaking of a new quality of life. The word *eternal* comes from *aiónios* and means age-long or unending. *Aiónios* certainly conveys the quantity of time, but it also carries with it the quality of a particular age. It can mean the unique reality of God's life in the soul of a person or God's life at work in the believer. Thus, believers who have eternal life are those who experience the quality of God's life now as a present possession. To have eternal life is to have a brand-new quality of life. This means that the believer will have abundant life (John 10:10). This means they will have new life (John 3:3). This means they will have a new quality of life (John 3:16). This means that Christians will be swimming upstream rather than floating downstream with the world and false religion. The Christian will have lost their life to gain it. What once was up is now down. The world's way will be seen as the wrong way and Christ's way as the only way. This is the paradox of losing your life to find it in Christ and the foolishness of holding on to one's life, but losing it eternally.

> *For what will it profit a man if he gains the whole world and forfeits his soul? Or what shall a man give in return for his soul?*
>
> —Matthew 16:26

Jesus is calling for everyone to do a spiritual assessment. Since there are two options that will account for one's spiritual destiny, this decision will require the utmost diligence. In other words, do a hypothetical spiritual equation. If you could have all the money in the world, become king over every nation, own all the land, own every possession, and control the whole world system, what good would this be if you lost your soul and went to hell? If you could gain the approval of all mankind but not have the approval of God, what would you have gained? If you could gain everything the world has to offer for a finite period, but ultimately lost your soul and went to hell for all eternity, what have you gained? If you could be lord of your life for a few years, but lost it forever, what would you have profited? The fact of the matter is that you'll never own the whole world. You'll never control the world system. Jesus posed an impossible hypothetical question to his audience. You'll never be king over every nation. You'll never own everything in the world, but even if you could, what you have profited if you eternally forfeited your soul? Only a fool would hang on to creation and forsake the Creator. Only a fool would serve money rather than the Master. Only a fool would serve immorality rather than Immanuel. Only a fool would serve sexual licentiousness rather than the Sovereign Lord. Only a fool would serve a job rather than Jesus. Only a fool would serve the self rather than the Savior. Only a fool would serve a false Christianity rather than follow Christ. Only a fool would serve "me" rather than the Messiah.

Not only do you need to do a spiritual accounting, but you should also do an assessment on your soul. Jesus asks, "*What shall a man give in return for his soul?*" In other words, what could possibly be more valuable than one's own soul? The obvious answer is that there is absolutely nothing that could be more valuable than one's own soul, nor is there anything on earth that can be given in exchange for one's soul. This is clearly a call to saving faith. Jesus declares that the eternity of one's soul is at stake. What can a man give in exchange for his soul? The answer is nothing. The soul is the most valuable thing that any person has. The life and soul of an individual is what Jesus is calling for. This is one of the clearest calls to saving faith in Christ. There are several ways one could paraphrase these verses:

- If anyone would come to Me and desire salvation, let him deny himself; let him die to himself and follow Me daily. For what would it profit a man if he kept his life, but lost his soul?

- If anyone would come to Me and desire to enter the kingdom of heaven, let him repudiate himself, mortify himself, and follow Me wherever I go. For if you maintain your position as lord of your life, you will lose it, but if you lose your life for My sake and the gospel, you will save your soul.

These verses are some of the clearest verses on Christ's call to a submissive and obedient faith in Him. We should see that this is clearly a gospel call to saving faith as the individual's response to Jesus determines whether they lose or save their soul.

So how is one to respond to the person and work of the Lord Jesus Christ, save their soul, enter the kingdom of heaven through the narrow gate, be loosed from their sin, and not forfeit their soul? Deny yourself, take up your cross, and follow the Lord Jesus Christ! Repent and believe the gospel (Mark 1:15). This is the only hope of the adulteress and adulterer. In the father's great wisdom, he can show his son that the Lord is the Savior of those who are sick and in need of a physician (Luke 5:32). The father can show his son that the Lord is willing and able to save the sexually immoral, adulterers, homosexuals, and fornicators (1 Corinthians 6:9–11). The father can show the son that the Lord is willing to wash, sanctify, and justify the worst of sinners. The gospel is the only hope for the adulterer, the adulteress, the homosexual, the porn-enslaved sinner, the fornicator, and all mankind enslaved to sin.

This is the gospel call that needs to ring forth. We are to urge men to be reconciled to God through Christ (2 Corinthians 5:20). We are to compel and constrain men to receive and accept this gospel call (Luke 14:23). We are to exhort men to agonize, strive, struggle, and fight to enter through the narrow gate because the time is short (Luke 13:24). We are to leave men with no hope of salvation other than repentance and faith in the Lord Jesus Christ. Hope for salvation in water baptism, chrismation, the Lord's Supper, sacraments, good works, or anything else is damning.

Fathers teach your sons about sexual sin. Teach your sons who God really is. Teach your sons about the horrors of hell. Teach your sons about the person and work of Christ. Teach your sons to repent and believe in the Lord Jesus Christ. Teach your sons the good news of the gospel of Jesus Christ—the only hope of salvation for the sinner!

Turn your eyes upon Jesus
Look full in His wonderful face
And the things of earth will grow strangely dim
In the light of His glory and grace.
Helen Howarth Lemmel (1922)

Notes

1 "Ralph Waldo Emerson Quotes," Goodreads, accessed December 11, 2025, https://www.goodreads.com/quotes/416934-sow-a-thought-and-you-reap-an-action-sow-an.

2 John Macarthur, "Sanctification and Sins of the Mind," sermon at Grace Community Church (Sun Valley, California), January 15, 2014.

3 John Macarthur, "Sanctification and Sins of the Mind," sermon at Grace Community Church (Sun Valley, California), January 15, 2014.

4 MacArthur, "Abstaining from Sexual Sin, Part 1," sermon at Grace Community Church (Sun Valley, California), August 12, 1990.

5 Zac Poonen, "Four Things to Flee From," sermon at CFC Church (Bangalor, India), August 20, 2014.

6 MacArthur, "Hacking Agag to Pieces" (Grace to You, 2022), 13.

7 John Owen quoted in MacArthur, "Hacking Agag to Pieces," 1.

8 MacArthur, "Hacking Agag to Pieces," 15.

9 MacArthur, "Hacking Agag to Pieces," 23–24.

10 MacArthur, "Hacking Agag to Pieces," 24.

11 MacArthur, "Hacking Agag to Pieces," 24.

12 MacArthur, "Hacking Agag to Pieces," 25.

13 Martyn Lloyd-Jones quoted in MacArthur, "Hacking Agag to Pieces," 26.

14 MacArthur, "Hacking Agag to Pieces," 26.

15 Tim Conway, "Evangelism: A Matter of Repentance and Faith," Grace Community Church, San Antonio, Texas, April 26, 2016.

16 Conway, "The Power of the Offensive Cross," Grace Community Church, San Antonio, Texas, February 14, 2010.

17 Charles Spurgeon, "Tetelestai–Paid in Full, " Precept Austin, November 7, 2022, https://www.preceptaustin.org/tetelestai-paid_in_full.

18 A. W. Pink, "Tetelestai–Paid in Full, " Precept Austin, November 7, 2022, https://www.preceptaustin.org/tetelestai-paid_in_full.

19 A. C. Gaebelein, "Tetelestai–Paid in Full, " Precept Austin, November 7, 2022, https://www.preceptaustin.org/tetelestai-paid_in_full.

20 Conway, "Evangelism: A Matter of Repentance and Faith," Grace Community Church, San Antonio, Texas, April 26, 2016.

21 John Foxe, *Foxe's Book of Martyrs* (JB Smith, 1856), 54.

22 Ibid.

23 Ibid.

24 Foxe, *Foxe's Book of Martyrs* (JB Smith, 1856), 55.

25 Foxe, *Foxe's Book of Martyrs* (JB Smith, 1856), 106–107.

26 Spurgeon, "Charles Spurgeon Quotes," Goodreads, accessed 12/21/2015, https://www.goodreads.com/quotes/989737-there-are-no-crown-bearers-in-heaven-that-were-not-cross-bearers.

About the Author

Curtis Braun is a reformed Christian author who has published such books as *The False Gospel of Baptismal Regeneration in the Lutheran Church and Christ's Call to Saving Faith,* and *The Portrait of the Preaching Pastor who Pleases the Lord.* In this book, Curtis seeks to exposit Proverbs 7 and demonstrate the Biblical mandate for fathers, parents, pastors, and the church to instruct and warn of the dangers of sexual sin and the need for the only Savior, the Lord Jesus Christ.

Additional Books by this author

The Portrait of the Preaching Pastor who Pleases the Lord

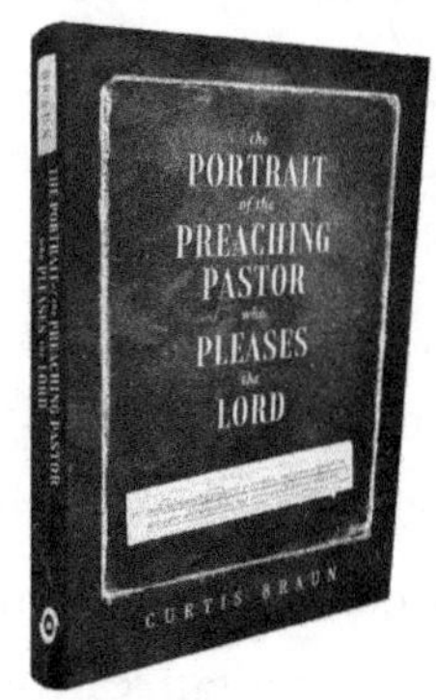

God has graciously given the church gifted men to feed, guide, and protect His people—to equip the saints, build up the body of Christ, and lead her toward spiritual maturity. Through their faithful ministry, the church is anchored in truth and guarded against deception.

Yet in many places, the high calling of the pastor has been diminished. Qualifications are watered down, biblical responsibilities are neglected, and the role is reshaped to suit personal ambitions. Some claim the title of evangelist while advancing sacramental traditions. Others gain followers and wealth but lack the character and integrity that Scripture demands. Still others stand behind pulpits to deliver lectures rather than preach the Word with conviction.

In light of these distortions, this book aims to recover a biblical vision of the pastoral office—one that honors God by presenting a faithful, scripturally grounded portrait of the man called to shepherd Christ's church.

The Apostle Paul's Theology on Conversion – and His Refutation and Condemnation of Sacramental Conversion and Salvation

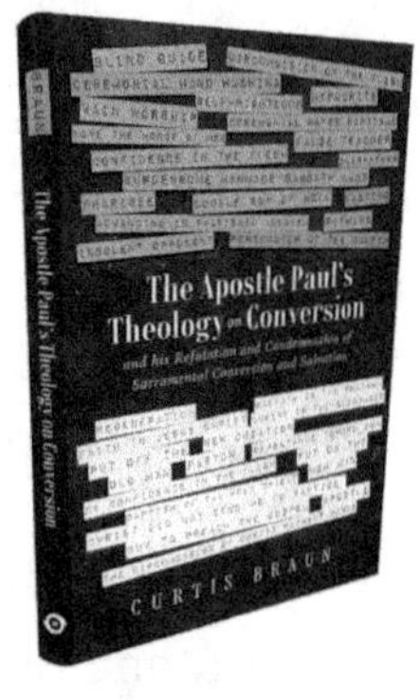

Sacramental conversion and salvation is a false gospel which is ubiquitous in the Catholic, Lutheran, Eastern Orthodox, Episcopalian, Anglican and many more churches. The apostle Paul is falsely proof-texted and caricatured as teaching conversion, regeneration, and salvation by sacraments while biblical consideration of his preconversion life as a ritualistic Jewish Pharisee is willfully neglected.

This book will explain prominent Jewish ceremonial rituals and observances, demonstrate their corruption during Paul's life, and show Paul's rejection and repentance from ceremonial-based salvation and condemnation of sacramental salvation. Paul proclaimed the reconciling gospel call of repentance towards God and faith in the Lord Jesus Christ.

www.ingramcontent.com/pod-product-compliance
Lightning Source LLC
LaVergne TN
LVHW010616100826
845148LV00014B/2994
* 9 7 9 8 9 0 3 4 4 0 1 0 8 *